Speaking in Shakespeare's Voice

Speaking in Shakespeare's Voice

A GUIDE FOR AMERICAN ACTORS

LINDA GATES

NORTHWESTERN UNIVERSITY PRESS

EVANSTON, ILLINOIS

Northwestern University Press
www.nupress.northwestern.edu

Printed in Canada
10 9 8 7 6 5 4 3 2 1

Library of Congress Cataloging-in-Publication Data

Names: Gates, Linda, author.
Title: Speaking in Shakespeare's voice : a guide for American actors / Linda
    Gates.
Description: Evanston, Illinois : Northwestern University Press,
    2019. | Includes bibliographical references.
Identifiers: LCCN 2018060498 | ISBN 9780810139909 (paper text : alk.
    paper) | ISBN 9780810139916 (e-book)
Subjects: LCSH: Shakespeare, William, 1564–1616—Dramatic
    production—Handbooks, manuals, etc. | Shakespeare, William, 1564–
    1616—Language—Handbooks, manuals, etc. | Acting—Handbooks,
    manuals, etc.
Classification: LCC PR3091 .G38 2018 | DDC 792.028—dc23
LC record available at https://lccn.loc.gov/2018060498

Thou speak'st aright;
I am that merry wanderer of the night.
—A Midsummer Night's Dream, 2.1.44–45

CONTENTS

ACKNOWLEDGMENTS

Every actor who wants to perform Shakespeare's great texts begins his or her training by building on the techniques learned by generations of actors who have struggled with the same challenge: how to perform the language of a more than four-hundred-year-old text, written in verse or highly stylized prose, and to communicate it so that the audience can both hear and understand it. Styles of acting change, but the words don't, and the task is the same.

The core of this book grew out of my early acting training at Carnegie Mellon University—then the Carnegie Institute of Technology—where as a young actor I began to explore how to perform Shakespeare's text with voice and speech teachers Edith Skinner and Margaret Prendergast McLean and acting teachers Mary Morris and Charlie Moore; and then at San Francisco State University, working with Jules Irving, Paul Rebillot, and Tom Tyrrell. I was equally fortunate that my first professional acting job at the San Francisco Actor's Workshop, under the artistic direction of Herbert Blau and Jules Irving, was performing Bianca in *The Taming of the Shrew*. That was when I began to discover that everything you need to know about character development and speaking the text can be found right there in the text if you look for it.

I'm especially grateful to the late Ted Hoffman, one of the founders of the NYU Tisch School of the Arts, who hired me right out of school to teach voice and speech as the assistant to Nora Dunfee, then head of speech and text, who gave me the opportunity to work for a year on training in voice with Kristin Linklater, whose work opened up new areas of vocal training for actors. All of our work in theater voice stands on the shoulders of those who have gone before: Edith Skinner, Margaret Prendergast McLean, Kristin Linklater, Patsy Rodenberg, Marjorie Phillips, Cecily Berry, Andrew Wade, the late Dorothy Run Mennen, and my colleagues at VASTA.

I am also indebted to Michael Khan, former artistic director of the Shakespeare Theatre Company in Washington, D.C., who first hired me to coach actors at the American Shakespeare Theatre in Stratford, Connecticut. I worked with the late British voice teacher Margery Phillips, then head of voice at the Yale School of Drama, who introduced me to an entirely new way of approaching voice and text. I want to give a special thanks to Moni Yakim and the late Alvin Epstein, who asked me to do the vocal scoring for their production of *The Tempest* at the Yale Repertory Theatre.

The core of this book grew out of teaching acting students both in America—at NYU Tisch SOA, Yale School of Drama, Circle in the Square Theatre School, the M.F.A. program at the Alabama Shakespeare Festival, University of Illinois Urbana–Champaign, and Northwestern University—and in England, at the Royal Central School of Speech and Drama and the BADA Midsummer in Oxford program.

As a vocal coach for Shakespeare's text, I am also indebted to Martin Platt, artistic director of the Alabama Shakespeare Festival, and especially to Barbara Gaines, artistic director of the Chicago Shakespeare Theater, who introduced me to the work of the First Folio and brought me in as vocal coach for her production of *Love's Labour's Lost*.

I am especially indebted to George Hall, who was head of the Acting course at the Royal Central School of Speech and Drama. George brought me to Central to teach voice in the Acting course, where I had the experience of working with the brilliant teachers in that program, including voice teachers Julia Wilson Dixon and Jane Cowell. George Hall had a unique approach to voice training, believing that all actors should be able to sing, and he introduced musical theater training and singing as part of the regular acting program. All of the acting students were expected to sing as well as to perform Shakespeare. I'll never forget the young Natasha Richardson performing in rotating repertory in her third year the title role in *The Duchess of Malfi* in the afternoon and then a role in the musical *Sweet Charity* that evening.

George Hall was also instrumental in my joining the distinguished faculty at the BADA Midsummer in Oxford program, where for more than sixteen years I had the opportunity to work with such great British theater professionals as John Barton, Julian Glover,

Diana Quick, Andrew Wade, John Gorrie, George Hall, John Jones, Lynn Farleigh, Jackie Snow, David Leveaux, Jane Lapotaire, Estelle Kohler, Richard Cottrell, and Michael Pennington.

Also, a special thanks to John Jones, who was an acting tutor and director at the Royal Central School of Speech and Drama, and who came to NYU at the invitation of Zelda Fitchandler to introduce Shakespeare training at NYU Tisch SOA. John's work on Shakespeare's text is so important to the work that I do, and I am so grateful for his help in choosing the monologues and scenes in the appendix.

I am also very grateful to my former Northwestern student Alan Paul, who is now associate artistic director at the Shakespeare Theatre Company in Washington, D.C. Alan interviewed their dramaturg for me about the company's choice of Shakespeare's texts.

I would also like to acknowledge the work of Guy Roberts, artistic director and founder of the Prague Shakespeare Company, who responded to my email inquiry in 2015 and has now established the company's Summer Shakespeare Intensive, the first Shakespeare training programs in English in the Czech Republic. In talking about Shakespeare training, Guy Roberts says:

> In Shakespeare, language is character. For the theater of Shakespeare's time it is not what you do as in our modern tradition but what you say and how you say it that defines who you are as a human being. Language for Shakespeare is the gateway into the human psyche and experience.

It is exciting to be a part of bringing Shakespeare in English to the cultural heart of Europe.

Publishing a book of this kind requires enormous effort on all levels. I would first like to thank Gianna Mosser, editor in chief at Northwestern University Press, who, when the book languished, reached out and put it on track. A grateful thanks to Jessica Marie Hinds-Bond, who took my final manuscript, which had collapsed into incoherence under the strain of three or four upgrades of Microsoft Word, and pulled it into coherence. I also thank Liz Hamilton, copyright librarian at Northwestern University Library, for advice on copyright and public domain, and my wonderful editors Anne Gendler and Mary Klein. Special thanks to Ramón H. Rivera-Servera, chair of Northwestern's Department of Theatre, who was my advocate and supported my application for a publication subvention grant; to my fellow colleagues on the Acting faculty; and to Northwestern theater historian Dassia Posner, for her good advice and encouragement. A very special thanks to the Kaplan Institute for the Humanities Publication Subvention Grant for helping me finish the book; to Eric Rasmussen, Shakespeare scholar and editor of the Royal Shakespeare Company's *Complete Works of William Shakespeare*, who introduced me to two of his Ph.D. students, Ian H. De Jong and Elsa L. De Jong, who volunteered to format and attribute all the Shakespeare selections in this book. Ian also introduced me to Open Source Shakespeare and its links to the world of the nineteenth-century Cambridge scholars George Aldis Wright and George Clark, the editors of the 1863 Cambridge Shakespeare and Globe editions of Shakespeare. Ian is an associate editor for the second edition of the Royal Shakespeare Company's *Complete Works of William Shakespeare*. Elsa De Jong's scholarship is focused on visual culture in early modern and eighteenth-century literature, and she teaches at the University of Reno.

My heartfelt thanks to the eminent Shakespeare scholar David Crystal, whose *Shakespeare's Words* was a special source for this book and who graciously responded to email questions throughout the process. David is one of the foremost experts on Shakespeare's Original Pronunciation, and in the summer of 2017 was consultant in residence for the Prague Shakespeare Summer Intensive and tirelessly advised the company on how to speak Shakespeare's text in OP.

I would like to offer a very special thanks to former Marine reservist Eric M. Johnson, who was called up with his fellow Marines to join in fighting the Iraq War. Eric, after the end of combat operations, used his time in the desert of Kuwait to build Open Source Shakespeare, a free and accessible website that is the source of all the Shakespeare selections in this book and a resource for Shakespeare lovers all over the world. *Semper Fi.*

A special thanks to my husband, George W. Tiller, whose endless patience, love, and encouragement kept me on track.

Finally, actors and directors can sometimes forget that our audience can be as passionate about Shakespeare as we are. Such an audience member was my dear friend John Mosedale, a wonderful journalist at CBS News for more than thirty-four years, who died at the age of eighty-four, after a heroic battle with cancer.

John loved Shakespeare passionately. He read and reread his plays constantly, saw every production he could, whenever he could, wherever he could, and wrote reviews for *The Shakespeare Newsletter*. John used to say, "Not a day of my life passes that I don't think of Shakespeare, and it is a rare and wasted day when I do not read something by him." In retirement he wrote a novel, *The Church of Shakespeare*, in which he wrote passionately about what Shakespearean actors do:

> You created shadows more solid than our substance. The Verona of the star-crossed lovers, the enchanted isle full of noises and sweet airs, the fog-shrouded castle at Elsinore, the blasted heath . . . the events and the people you portrayed, are now hard-wired in our hearts and, in the mysterious manner of Shakespeare, will become more familiar as it recedes.

Speaking in Shakespeare's Voice

Note about Quotations from Shakespeare

All Shakespeare quotations are from Open Source Shakespeare at www.opensourceshakespeare.org unless otherwise noted. The line numbers provided correspond roughly to those in print editions of Shakespeare and are there to help those who may be using such editions, since no two are exactly alike. Open Source Shakespeare features both basic and advanced text search features that make it easy to locate a quotation by using a key word or two or a phrase.

Introduction

Shakespeare in America

It is surprising that even now, in the early part of the twenty-first century, when America can boast of having over 275 Shakespeare theaters of varying sizes performing the plays of William Shakespeare to enthusiastic audiences, the reality is that some American actors are still uncertain about how to perform Shakespeare's text. Some may have had a bad experience reading it in high school, where they found the plays full of archaic words and written in verse that sometimes rhymed and sometimes didn't, or in prose that almost sounded like verse. They may have been further discouraged by listening to their fellow students read Shakespeare aloud, word by tortuous word. In college, they may have studied Shakespeare with professors in the English department who approached the text as literature rather than as a script for actors. Or if they were in an acting class in a theater department, they may not have had any classes in how to approach the text in terms of speaking or how the text helps the actor in performance. As actors they may have worked with directors whose approach to Shakespeare's plays was to apply techniques such as improvisation to the rehearsal process, a technique more suited to acting in naturalistic twentieth century plays than to the plays of Shakespeare, who wrote according to the principles of Elizabethan rhetoric. Under these circumstances it is understandable that many actors are overwhelmed and decide that speaking Shakespeare's text is the province of classically trained British actors and beyond the skills of ordinary American actors.

The purpose of this book is to help all actors, but especially American actors, build the vocal skills and confidence necessary to speak Shakespeare's text and to communicate it to an audience. It covers the basic elements of vocal production, including breath, vocal placement and resonance, and the sounds and principles of Standard American English voice and diction—always using Shakespeare's text as a practical guide. It also acquaints the actor with a working knowledge of some of the basic principles of Elizabethan rhetoric and verse speaking found in Shakespeare's plays and how modern actors can apply those principles in performance today.

Shakespearean Acting in Early America

For American actors unfamiliar with the history of performance of Shakespeare in America, it can be helpful to look back at some of the ways in which British and American actors originally approached the performance of Shakespeare's plays in the new land, and how the two approaches began to seem to be different.

In 1607, when the first permanent English settlers arrived in Jamestown, in what is now the state of Virginia, it is possible that some of them might have had direct experience seeing Shakespeare's plays at the Globe Theatre in London. In the same year that they set sail for the New World, the following plays were being performed at the Globe: *King Lear*, *Measure for Measure*, *Macbeth*, *Antony and Cleopatra*, and *All's Well That Ends Well*.

However, in 1620, when the Pilgrims—or Puritans, as they were then called in England—arrived in New England, it is doubtful that any of them were regular theatergoers in London or anywhere else, because their strongly held religious beliefs were not sympathetic to theater in any form. In fact the Puritans were responsible for closing all the theaters in England in 1642.

It wasn't until 1723 that a company headed by Walter Murray and Thomas Kean presented a production of *Richard III* in Williamsburg, Virginia.[1] Other companies soon followed and were established in other American cities where performances of Shakespeare's plays were a regular part of their repertoire.

When George Washington was a member of the House of Burgesses in Williamsburg, Virginia, long before he became commander of the American forces in the American Revolution, he was an avid theatergoer. He is reported to have enjoyed the English comedies

The School for Scandal, *The Recruiting Officer*, and *The Beaux Strat-agem*, and to have attended productions of *The Tempest* and *Hamlet* at a theater in Williamsburg. According to one of his biographers, Ron Chernow, Washington's papers contained many references to Shakespeare, particularly the Roman plays and the history plays. There are also many references to *Othello*, *Macbeth*, *The Merchant of Venice*, and *The Tempest*.[2]

When the French writer Alexis de Tocqueville was traveling through the new nation in 1831, gathering material for what would become his seminal book *Democracy in America*, he commented on the popularity of Shakespeare among even the poorest citizens: "There is scarcely a pioneer's cabin where one does not encounter some odd volumes of Shakespeare. I recall having read the feudal drama of *Henry V* for the first time in a *log-house*."[3]

British Acting in Early America

After the American Revolution, most performances of Shakespeare's plays were still being performed by British actors, who crossed the Atlantic to take advantage of the growing number of venues provided by the new republic with its quickly expanding territories. One of these British actors, John Bernard, wrote a book about his experience titled *Retrospections of America, 1797–1811*, in which he said, "If an actor were unemployed, want and shame were not before him: he had merely to visit some town in the interior where no theater existed, but 'read-ings' were permitted; and giving a few recitations from Shakespeare and Sterne, his pockets in a night or two were amply replenished."[4]

One of the most celebrated of the British visitors was the actor Edmund Kean, whose tour of America in 1820 was greeted with wild enthusiasm by audiences and, as one critic reported, "I know but few persons, and I am not of the number, who hesitate to acknowl-edge that Mr. Kean may be styled an extraordinary actor. . . . He ought to be seen by the Americans who are amateurs or would be connoisseurs in the affairs of the stage."[5]

Unfortunately, after extensive touring throughout the former col-onies and performing to great acclaim and sold-out houses, Kean misjudged the temper of some American audiences, who hadn't quite forgotten the animosity stirred up during the second war between Britain and America in 1812, when British troops burned the White

House. In May, before sailing home to England, Kean decided to make one more appearance in Boston. It was late in the season and his manager tried to persuade him to postpone his appearance until the fall, but Kean insisted that an actor of his caliber should be able to fill the house in any season. After playing *King Lear* to a mediocre house the first night and to a half-full house the second, Kean arrived at the theater for a third night's performance of *Richard III* to find a mostly empty house and arrogantly refused to perform, declaring that he would not play to the bare walls and leaving the theater.[6] When some newspapers reported that he was said to have made disparaging remarks about Americans, his subsequent performances were greeted with catcalls and unruly behavior. He quickly fled back to the safety of England.

The First American-British Acting Rivalry

In the early nineteenth century, the American-born actor Edwin Forrest, who had begun his acting career in America, sailed to England where he performed Shakespearean roles on tour throughout Britain to some acclaim. He then returned to America to establish himself as the first American Shakespearean actor. Said one critic: "Mr. Forrest is not to be judged by the ordinary canonical standards of criticism, at least on his native soil. He has created a school in his art, strictly American, and he stands forth as the very embodiment, as it were, of *the masses* of American character."[7]

When the noted British actor William Macready, who was known for his more dignified, declamatory style as compared to Edwin Forrest's more passionate, spontaneous approach, arrived in the United States on tour, their rivalry, inflamed and encouraged by sensational reports in the press, was intense. In the spring of 1849, the two actors appeared simultaneously in New York performing in the title role of *Macbeth*. Edwin Forrest had developed a huge following among the working classes for his fiery, emotional delivery, while William Macready was the favorite of the upper classes, who admired his more cerebral style. There was intense debate as to who was the better Shakespearean actor, British or American.

At one of Macready's performances the audience shouted and jeered, pelting the stage with rotten eggs. Discouraged by his reception, Macready wanted to close the production, but his upper-class patrons begged him to continue and promised support and protection. On the night of May 10, an angry mob of over twenty thousand lower-class fans of Edwin Forrest gathered outside the Astor Place Theatre, where Macready was performing before an upper-class audience.

Led by supporters of Edwin Forrest, riots broke out in front of the theater. After police were unable to contain the violence, the authorities were forced to call out the militia. When the soldiers arrived, they were set upon by the outraged mob, and the soldiers finally fired into the crowd, killing at least twenty-two people and wounding over 150. Certainly, a low point in British and American theater relations.[8]

Black American Actors and Shakespeare

Performing Shakespeare was not limited to white Americans. Ira Frederick Aldridge, one of the first African American actors, was born in New York in 1807 to free black parents and became interested in theater while attending the African Free School in New York. Aldridge made his debut as an actor in the city's first African American theater group, at the African Grove Theatre. This theater, founded by William Brown, produced *Othello* and *Richard III* in addition to other plays. After it closed in 1823, Aldridge emigrated to England, where black actors in the nineteenth century had far greater opportunities than in America, where slavery was still legal in the southern states.

Shortly after arriving in England, Aldridge moved to Glasgow, Scotland, where he studied at the University of Glasgow and refined his voice and dramatic skills in theater. Afterward, he moved to London and made his debut in October 1825 in the role of Prince Oroonoko of Africa in the melodrama *The Revolt of Surinam, or A Slave's Revenge* at the Royal Coburg Theatre (now the Old Vic). He took to billing himself as the "African Roscius," a title alluding to Quintus Roscius Gallus, an eminent Roman actor of comedy and tragedy and a former slave who had tutored Cicero. The theater world of that day had adopted the name as an appellation signifying extraordinary dramatic ability.

Aldridge's major break came when Edmund Kean (the same Edmund Kean who had such trouble with unruly audiences in Boston), who was starring as Othello, collapsed during a performance at Covent Garden in March 1833. Aldridge was asked to fill the role for the rest of the play's run. His performance earned a mixed reception from the London theater critics, who objected to his race, his youth, and his inexperience, and there were accusations that proslavery business interests had bribed the reviewers.[9] However, it was a role he would remain associated with until his death.

Afterward, Aldridge toured extensively throughout Britain and Europe, honing and developing his craft. He was especially popular in Prussia and Russia, where he received top honors from heads of state. He became a British citizen in 1863 and is the only African American actor among the first thirty-three actors of the English stage honored with bronze plaques at the Royal Shakespeare Theatre in Stratford-upon-Avon. He died while on tour in Europe in August 1867 and is buried in Lodz, Poland.[10]

Shakespeare in Pioneer America

As settlers began to move west and into the interior of the country, Shakespeare's *Collected Works* along with the King James Bible continued to be the most popular books found in American homes. During the California gold rush of the 1840s, miners whiled away the harsh winter months by sitting around campfires and acting out Shakespeare's plays from memory. According to American journalist Karl Knortz, who emigrated from Germany at age twenty-two, writing in the 1880s, "There is, assuredly, no other country on earth in which Shakespeare and the Bible are held in such general high esteem."[11] Even pioneer settlers, some of whom couldn't read or write, would show up to see touring Shakespeare companies, who sometimes traveled down the Mississippi on flat-bottom boats performing Shakespeare's plays at boat landings along the way until they reached New Orleans, where the performers would sell their boats then travel upriver to start over again.

In Mark Twain's *Adventures of Huckleberry Finn*, the two con men—the king and the duke—disguise themselves as famous British actors David Garrick the Younger and Edmund Kean the Elder, and plan to present a performance of excerpts from *Hamlet* and *Romeo and Juliet*, which they said they retained from memory, as a way of hoodwinking the town. They are convinced that a performance of Shakespeare is just the way to attract an audience and make some easy money. Here is Huckleberry Finn describing their deliberations:

After dinner the duke says:

"Well, Capet, we'll want to make this a first-class show, you know, so I guess we'll add a little more to it. We want a little something to answer encores with, anyway."

"What's onkores, Bilgewater?"

The duke told him, and then says:

"I'll answer by doing the Highland fling or the sailor's hornpipe; and you—well, let me see—oh, I've got it—you can do Hamlet's soliloquy."

"Hamlet's which?"

"Hamlet's soliloquy, you know; the most celebrated thing in Shakespeare. Ah, it's sublime, sublime! Always fetches the house. I haven't got it in the book—I've only got one volume—but I reckon I can piece it out from memory. I'll just walk up and down a minute, and see if I can call it back from recollection's vaults."

So he went to marching up and down, thinking, and frowning horrible every now and then; then he would hoist up his eyebrows; next he would squeeze his hand on his forehead and stagger back and kind of moan; next he would sigh, and next he'd let on to drop a tear. It was beautiful to see him. By and by he got it. He told us to give attention. Then he strikes a most noble attitude, with one leg shoved forwards, and his arms stretched away up, and his head tilted back, looking up at the sky; and then he begins to rip and rave and grit his teeth; and after that, all through his speech, he howled, and spread around, and swelled up his chest, and just knocked the spots out of any acting ever *I* see before. This is the speech—I learned it, easy enough, while he was learning it to the king:

To be, or not to be; that is the bare bodkin
That makes calamity of so long life;
For who would fardels bear, till Birnam Wood do come to
    Dunsinane,
But that the fear of something after death
Murders the innocent sleep,
Great nature's second course,
And makes us rather sling the arrows of outrageous fortune
Than fly to others that we know not of.
There's the respect must give us pause:
Wake Duncan with thy knocking! I would thou couldst;

For who would bear the whips and scorns of time,
The oppressor's wrong, the proud man's contumely,
The law's delay, and the quietus which his pangs might take,
In the dead waste and middle of the night, when
    churchyards yawn
In customary suits of solemn black,
But that the undiscovered country from whose bourne no
    traveler returns,
Breathes forth contagion on the world,
And thus the native hue of resolution, like the poor cat i'
    the adage,
Is sicklied o'er with care,
And all the clouds that lowered o'er our housetops,
With this regard their currents turn awry,
And lose the name of action.
'Tis a consummation devoutly to be wished.
But soft you, the fair Ophelia:
Ope not thy ponderous and marble jaws,
But get thee to a nunnery—go![12]

At the end of three days of performance, the two con artists performing their Shakespeare pastiche made a handsome profit. According
to Huckleberry Finn, "Them rapscallions took in four hundred and
sixty-five dollars in that three nights. I never see money hauled in by
the wagon-load like that before."[13]

American Actresses and Shakespeare

American actresses also played a part in British and American
Shakespearean acting. Charlotte Cushman began her career as an
opera singer but suffered irreversible voice damage at a concert in
New Orleans due to singing roles outside her natural range. She was
then encouraged to become an actress.

Cushman was best known for the role of Lady Macbeth, which
she performed in New York with William Macready, the same British actor who had been the catalyst for the Astor Place Theatre riots.
Macready said of her, "The Miss Cushman who acted Lady Macbeth
interested me very much. She has to learn her art but she showed
mind and sympathy with me,—a novelty so refreshing to me on the

stage."[14] Urged by William Macready to go to London for further training, Cushman traveled to England, where she worked to improve her technique. A few years later, she played a command performance before Queen Victoria as Katherine in *Henry VIII*.

One of Charlotte Cushman's more fervent supporters was the poet and journalist Walt Whitman, who frequently wrote in his theater reviews of the superiority of American actors as opposed to their British counterparts. In an 1846 review, he proclaimed that Charlotte Cushman's "natural" style could not be "superceded by the fifth rate artistic trash that comes over to us from the old world," adding that "Miss Cushman assuredly bears away the palm from them all."[15]

Cushman continued to perform with great success in England and frequently returned to the American stage, where she commanded top dollar for her performances. She retired briefly from the theater and moved to Rome, where she lived with an expat community of writers, sculptors, painters, and other artists while still returning frequently to perform both in England and America.

In 1869 she was diagnosed with breast cancer and went to Scotland for surgery. Afterward, she returned to America, where, lacking the stamina for stage performances, she continued to perform dramatic readings of scenes from Shakespeare and poetry. At the time of her death in 1876, Cushman was hailed for her artistry and considered one of the most famous women in the world.

Abraham Lincoln and Shakespeare

As a young boy growing up on the Kentucky frontier, Abraham Lincoln began to learn to read with *Dilworth's Spelling-Book*, by the eighteenth-century English schoolmaster Thomas Dilworth. Used by generations of British and American schoolchildren, Dilworth's book featured stories and pictures of interest to children to illustrate grammar, spelling, and syntax, including examples in both prose and verse.

Lincoln's mother died shortly after the family moved to Indiana, and the following year his father married Sarah Bush Johnston, who brought with her a wonderful library containing such works as *The Arabian Nights*, *Robinson Crusoe*, Noah

Webster's *Speller*, Bunyan's *The Pilgrim's Progress*, and Lindley Murray's *English Reader*, as well as a good deal of poetry, including some of Shakespeare's most famous speeches, which Lincoln memorized and would often recite.

In addition to literature, Lincoln also loved the theater. The successful nineteenth-century actor Joseph Jefferson III, after whom the Chicago Jeff Awards were named, recalls in his memoirs how Lincoln, as a young lawyer in Springfield, Illinois, came to the defense of his father's theater. The threat of exorbitant licensing fees—due to political pressure exerted by a religious revival group in town—was preventing the theater from opening. According to Jefferson,

> [Lincoln] handled the subject with tact, skill, and humor,
> tracing the history of the drama from the time when Thes-
> pis acted in a cart to the stage of today. He illustrated his
> speech with a number of anecdotes, and kept the council in
> a roar of laughter; his good-humor prevailed, and the exor-
> bitant tax was taken off.[16]

Later, as president, Lincoln often went to Ford's Theatre, where he saw Shakespeare's plays and sometimes invited the actors to the White House to discuss their performances and interpretation of the characters. "He nearly knew Shakespeare by heart," a clerk once said of him.[17]

One famous story involves Lincoln writing to the actor James H. Hackett about his portrayal of Falstaff in Shakespeare's *Henry IV, Part 1*. Lincoln seemed concerned that the performance left out speeches that he knew well from his reading of Shakespeare's plays. According to Douglas L. Wilson's fascinating article "His Hour upon the Stage" in the *American Scholar*:

> Lincoln knew Shakespeare from his incessant reading and
> rereading of printed texts of the plays. . . . What Lincoln
> probably didn't know until he began seeing the same plays
> performed on the Washington stage . . . is that the texts
> of the acting editions used for theatrical performances in

Lincoln's day were different from the texts found in editions intended for readers, and in some cases substantially different.[18]

According to Wilson, "It helps us understand what [Lincoln] once told his friend Noah Brooks after seeing Edwin Booth perform in *The Merchant of Venice*: 'It was a good performance but I had a thousand times rather read it at home.' "

Barry Edelstein, author of *Bardisms: Shakespeare for All Occasions*, tells a story about Lincoln and Shakespeare where John Forney, secretary of the Senate, was visiting the White House toward the end of the Civil War and came upon Lincoln asleep at his desk with his copy of Shakespeare in front of him. Lincoln woke suddenly and "immediately read aloud" Macbeth's soliloquy:

> To-morrow, and to-morrow, and to-morrow,
> Creeps in this petty pace from day to day
> To the last syllable of recorded time,
> And all our yesterdays have lighted fools
> The way to dusty death. Out, out, brief candle!
> Life's but a walking shadow, a poor player
> That struts and frets his hour upon the stage
> And then is heard no more: it is a tale
> Told by an idiot, full of sound and fury,
> Signifying nothing.
>
> *Macbeth*, 5.5.21–30

After he had finished, "Lincoln told a stunned Forney that Macbeth's extreme nihilism and utter hopelessness 'comes to me tonight like a consolation.' "[19]

Shakespearean Acting in America Today

The American actor Nicolas Cage has said that he doesn't think American actors can perform Shakespeare because it doesn't sound right to him:

I'm one of those people that feel that Americans shouldn't do Shakespeare. The manner of the English speech seems to work effortlessly with William Shakespeare but with Americans it seems stuck.[20]

What does he mean? Is he saying that Shakespeare can only be performed with a British accent?

British or American English for Performing Shakespeare?

Shakespeare and his actors would certainly have been astonished to hear most current productions of the Royal Shakespeare Company, with their dropped *r*'s before consonants and rounded tones. The English in Shakespeare's time consisted of strongly pronounced *r*'s and would have sounded almost Irish to our ears. It would certainly be much closer to spoken American English than British Received Pronunciation, or RP, which is standard British or, as it is sometimes called, BBC English. It was only after the American Revolution that the British use of the *ah* vowel in words like *bath*, *dance*, *ask*, *can't*, and *pass* became standard.

Trevor Nunn, an artistic director of the Royal Shakespeare Company, is quoted as saying, "It is almost certainly true that today's American accent is closer to the sounds that Shakespeare heard when he was writing."[21]

British versus American Actor Training for Shakespeare

As a voice and speech teacher, I have taught at numerous M.F.A. programs, including NYU Tisch School of the Arts and the Yale School of Drama in the United States and the Royal Central School of Speech and Drama in England. I have worked as a voice and text coach for several American Shakespeare companies, including the Alabama Shakespeare Festival, Chicago Shakespeare Theater, and the American Shakespeare Theatre, and with American directors such as Barbara Gaines at Chicago Shakespeare, Michael Kahn, Martin Platt, and Mary Zimmerman. For the past eighteen years, I have also taught both British and American actors at the British American Drama Academy's Midsummer in Oxford program, working with British voice teachers and British Shakespeare directors such as John Barton, John Jones, John Gorrie, David Giles, Stephen Hollis, and George Hall. This experience has led to some observations about the ways in which British and American training programs and actors approach Shakespeare that I would like to share with you.

When I began my acting training at Carnegie Mellon (then the Carnegie Institute of Technology), the emphasis on speaking Shakespeare, as taught by my teacher Edith Skinner, was on the sounds of Shakespeare's text and the accuracy of the sounds, which were supposed to be spoken with a "mid-Atlantic" accent. The term *mid-Atlantic* referred to a mythical continent halfway between England and America and reflected the way the inhabitants of this imaginary continent would be presumed to speak. It was really an extension of the way stage actors of the early part of the twentieth century spoke. A great many film stars of the period used this accent, including Cary Grant, Jane Wyatt, Grace Kelly, Joan Crawford, and Orson Welles, as well as stage actors such as Christopher Plummer, Agnes Moorehead, Kelsey Grammer, and Richard Chamberlain. Surprisingly, the accent is still often used today when a director would like to have a unified sound in a classic play.

On the other hand, some very fine Shakespearean directors don't seem to care whether the sounds are accurate or not. In England, there has been a steady move away from Received Pronunciation, and you can now hear a variety of regional accents even at the Royal Shakespeare Company.

When I taught in England, the chief difference, as exemplified by the work of John Barton, was that the focus was on the text and the ways in which the text focuses and helps the acting. In his book *Playing Shakespeare*, John Barton says,

> I believe that speech goes to the very heart of it. It's one of those utterances which seems a bit simple and limited at first, but if you live with it you will find that it begins to resonate and to open doors. I also believe that in the Elizabethan theatre the actors knew how to use and interpret the *hidden direction* Shakespeare himself provided in his verse and his prose.[22]

The directors and actors in Britain that I worked with did not eschew truth or emotion in their approach to acting Shakespeare, but their work was grounded very firmly on the text and how the actors should allow the text to support everything they did on stage.

Shakespeare, Stanislavsky, and the "Method"

The "Method" refers to the American adaptation of the work of the highly influential Russian theater director and teacher Konstantin Stanislavsky, as interpreted by Lee Strasberg at the Actors Studio and Stella Adler, Sanford Meisner, Bobby Lewis, Elia Kazan, and others. Stanislavsky's approach was highly influential in the work of the Group Theatre and has been used extensively in the training of American actors. It has also been blamed, unfairly in my view, for the poor diction and slovenly speech of some of its adherents.

Harold Clurman, one of America's greatest theater critics and directors as well as one of the founders of the Group Theatre, said regarding Stanislavsky's views on voice and diction:

> I have never heard anyone speak as long and as dogmatically on the importance of the voice and diction as did Stanislavsky to me on the several occasions of our meeting in Paris and Moscow. . . . The actress I most admired in his company was guilty of rather common speech and therefore could not gain his wholehearted approbation. . . . He was not satisfied that anybody anywhere had developed a voice to match the inherent demands of Shakespeare's verse.[23]

Stanislavsky wrote two books, *An Actor Prepares* and *Building a Character*, to set down his precepts about actor training, using a fictional acting student named Kostya as a way of embodying his approach. He intended *An Actor Prepares* to cover the actor's emotional approach to acting and *Building a Character* to address the technical aspects of body, movement, voice, diction, text, and physical characterization. Stanislavsky was in contact with an American publisher, and the two books were meant to be published together as a set.

At the outbreak of World War II, *An Actor Prepares* was finished and ready to be sent to the American publisher. However,

Stanislavsky was still working on *Building a Character*, which was unfinished and existed in several different versions.

During the war, mail service between the Soviet Union and the United States often broke down, and finally it became impossible to send the finished manuscript of *Building a Character*. It was almost fifteen years before the second volume of Stanislavsky's work was finally published in the United States. Meanwhile, based on the first book, the idea that the Stanislavsky system of acting didn't incorporate speech, voice, text, and movement had taken hold in some quarters and became a fixture in an American approach to performing Shakespeare.

Marlon Brando, Shakespeare, and the Method

As a young actor, Marlon Brando electrified the Broadway stage with his performance as Stanley Kowalski in Tennessee Williams's *A Streetcar Named Desire*. He was also a member of the Actors Studio and associated with the Method. According to Harold Clurman, the success of that characterization had much to do with the public ideas of method acting:

> It is worth mentioning that when I first heard that Brando was to do the part I thought he had been miscast. For I had known Brando, whom I had previously directed in a play by Maxwell Anderson, as an innately delicate, thoughtful and intellectually eager young man. No matter! For an alarming number of young people in the theatre Kowalski was Brando and Brando was great! . . . They equated the tough guy, delinquent aspect of the characterization with a heedlessness, a rebelliousness, a "freedom" and a kind of pristine strength which the performance seemed to them to symbolize. In it, they found combined their unconscious ideal: creative power in acting with a blind revolt against all sorts of conformity both in life and on the stage.[24]

When Marlon Brando was cast in the role of Mark Antony in the film *Julius Caesar* with such famous British Shakespearean actors as John Gielgud and James Mason, purists were aghast. How could the mumbling Stanley from *A Streetcar Named Desire* hold his own in one of Shakespeare's most demanding roles against these seasoned Shakespeareans? Fortunately, the film is available, and to my mind his performance is astonishing. I watched it again recently and not only did he speak clearly with good diction, but he was able to let the oration over the body of Caesar build to its peak and not pull back for lack of breath. He was nominated for an Academy Award for Best Actor in a leading role for his performance, and it is clear that mumbling was a style he had chosen for the role of Stanley Kowalski and not a speech impediment.

Interestingly, John Gielgud talks in his book *An Actor and His Time* about working with Marlon Brando on the text:

> I had only one scene with him in the film. We went through the speeches in the morning and he asked me "What do you think of the way I did those speeches?" So I went through them with him and made some suggestions. He thanked me very politely and went away. The next morning, when we shot the scene, I found that he had taken note of everything I had said and spoke the lines exactly as I had suggested. . . . I never met Brando again, which was a pity because I felt that he was enormously responsive.[25]

Performing Shakespeare in America Today

Much has changed over the last thirty years in terms of American actors and Shakespeare. There are Shakespeare theaters in every state of the union—including two in Alaska. In their 2006–2007 season, Chicago Shakespeare Theater even brought their highly acclaimed production of *Henry IV, Parts 1 and 2,* directed by founder Barbara Gaines, to the Royal Shakespeare Company, where it sold out. I remember standing outside the theater in Stratford-upon-Avon at intermission, listening to the British audience praise the production.

One man said: "The Yanks are really good!" Someone else marveled that they didn't sound like Al Capone. Michael Billington of the *Guardian* wrote,

> But the main pleasure lies in seeing these great plays done with such clarity. "This is no world to play with mammets," Hotspur admonishes his wife. Nor indeed, I felt, with Mamets, since these Chicago actors show themselves as much at home in the more taxing world of Shakespeare.[26]

British Actor Michael York on American Shakespeare

From the moment I came here in the late '60s, I was aware of this strange conception in America. Americans thought that we Brits had a lock on Shakespeare because of the way we sounded. I was always at pains to remind them that . . . the accent of Shakespeare's day with the Devon "rrrr" crossed over with the settlers and it took root in America. So if you want to hear—and the key word is *hear*—(the Elizabethans said "That we shall *hear* a play" not *see* one), if you want to hear an "authentic" performance, see it here in America! Don't go see it in Britain, where our accents have gone through this lunatic sound change with our German kings and our whatever. See it here in America, where you have preserved *purity*![27]

Performing Shakespeare in Britain Today

Since the opening of the replica of Shakespeare's Globe Theatre in London, on Bankside, not far from where the original Globe was located, there has been a movement to explore Shakespeare's original stagecraft, using Shakespeare's Globe as the laboratory. This has also extended to the use of OP, or Original Pronunciation, in performances of Shakespeare. In 2004, under the linguistic supervision of David Crystal, professor of linguistics at the University of Wales, an

OP performance of *Romeo and Juliet* took place that was a revelation for modern British audiences, who remarked that they could not only understand it, but that it seemed clearer than standard British RP for many. I happened to see the production and found that it sounded a bit Irish, a bit Northern England, and perhaps a little American, but certainly easily comprehensible. The following year Shakespeare's Globe performed *Troilus and Cressida* in OP, and productions of Shakespeare have been performed in OP in both America and Australia. In 2017, the Prague Shakespeare Company brought Professor Crystal in for a residency with their Summer Shakespeare Intensive to help the actors with their OP pronunciation for three productions, including *A Midsummer Night's Dream* with the fairies and the mechanicals speaking in OP and the rest of the cast speaking in standard American English. For the European actors in the cast and two students from New Zealand, it was a challenge, as some of them had learned British English in school and were unfamiliar with standard American sounds. Somehow Shakespeare managed to prevail. Perhaps both sides of the Atlantic are coming closer together linguistically.

I believe that audiences today remain as eager to see Shakespeare's plays as those audiences in early America who flocked to see touring companies of actors perform in town halls, on river boats, or in any space that would provide room for a crowd to gather and actors to perform. It is also an exciting time for young American actors, who may have been hesitant in the past but are now eager to rise to the challenge of performing Shakespeare's plays with the confidence that Shakespeare belongs to them as well as to the British. The purpose of this book is to encourage these young actors by giving them some of the tools they will need to speak his text and to be heard and understood by an audience.

1

Breathing for Shakespeare's Text

... give it breath with your mouth, and it will discourse most eloquent music.

—*Hamlet*, 3.2.355–56

There are a lot of theories involving breathing techniques for actors performing Shakespeare. One of them, attributed to the legendary British director Tyrone Guthrie, is that an actor should be able to speak twelve lines of Shakespeare on one breath. The Canadian actor William Hutt, who worked with Guthrie at the Stratford Shakespeare Festival in Canada, says that it was six lines on one breath.[1] Whether twelve lines or six, the larger question, it seems to me, is why? Why would being able to sustain six or twelve lines, on one breath, help the actor perform Shakespeare's text? Leaving aside whether Guthrie was right about the need for actors to speak twelve or six lines on one breath, or whether there might be a better way, why would he say it in the first place?

Shakespeare and Breath

Shakespeare's text is full of large images, large emotions, and large ideas, spoken within a structure of either prose or verse. The text requires enough breath to enable the actor to share all of this with an audience. Sometimes the thoughts are expressed in long phrases:

> when I shall die,
> Take him and cut him out in little stars,
> And he will make the face of heaven so fine
> That all the world will be in love with night
> And pay no worship to the garish sun.
>
> *Romeo and Juliet*, 3.2.19–23

Sometimes the phrases are short:

> we know what we are, but know not what we may be.
>
> *Hamlet*, 4.5.48

However long or short the structure or the line, an actor needs to be able to sustain that thought to the end of the phrase and not break it in the middle because he or she is out of breath.

Breath and Thought

The need to speak triggers the need to breathe. The breath and the thought occur as one action. This is especially true in performing Shakespeare's text, which has to convey complex and sometimes long thoughts to an audience. The thought provokes the breath, which fuels the ability to speak. The actor's job is to connect the breath to the thoughts and feelings of the characters in the text, while communicating this to an audience. While this process may change with different actors' interpretations of a character, the goal is still the same—the need to speak provokes the breath. This requires the actor to breathe in quickly and sustain the outgoing breath, while speaking the thought to the end of the line. Whether the phrase is long or short, the inhalation must still be quick—there isn't time to stop and pause and then breathe. Moreover, to pause for a breath in the middle of a verse line when there is no mark of punctuation breaks the thought and the action of the character.

Sustaining the Breath

The most efficient method of breathing is a combination of diaphragmatic and rib breathing. Because the intercostal muscles between the ribs are very elastic, the slight expansion of the ribs lowers the diaphragm, providing extra room for more air to enter the lungs to sustain the breath. The expansion of the lower ribs also opens the throat and seems to give extra richness of timbre to the lower tones of the voice. The thought provokes the impulse to breathe, which initiates the sound of the voice, which is then supported by the pressure of the breath behind the sound.

Catch Breath

A quick breath taken while speaking is called a *catch breath*, a short breath on top of the breath that you have already taken. There is no need to exhale before speaking the next line, and there is no need to stop and then breathe; just use a catch breath to get you to the next phrase where you can then take another catch breath. The catch breath has to become second nature, like a reflex. You can't stop to think about it.

The site of the catch breath is in the *solar plexus*, or epigastrium, which is not a muscle but a network of ganglia and nerves in the center of the abdomen, below the sternum in the center of the abdominal wall, where the diaphragm and the abdominal muscles meet. It can always be found at the location of a slight cough. When you are speaking and come to a pause, the muscle should automatically release for the breath to "top the tank," or to breathe on top of the breath you have already taken.

Exercise: **Catch Breath**

Place your hand on your midsection (where you cough) and begin to pant on *sh-sh-sh-sh* (IPA symbol ʃ), keeping a steady rhythm and letting your hand bounce with each breath. Practice maintaining the pant and then catching a breath at regular intervals, starting at 1-2 (breath), then 1-2-3 (breath), then 1-2-3-4-5-6 (breath), 1-2-3-4-5-6-7-8-9-10 (breath), 1-2-3-4-5-6-7-8-9-10-11-12 (breath), building up to 1-20. The intake of air should be quick and silent, and the outgoing breath long and sustained.

ʃ-ʃ (breath) ʃ-ʃ (breath) ʃ-ʃ (breath) ʃ-ʃ (breath)
ʃ-ʃ-ʃ (breath) ʃ-ʃ-ʃ (breath)
ʃ-ʃ-ʃ-ʃ-ʃ-ʃ (breath) ʃ-ʃ-ʃ-ʃ-ʃ-ʃ (breath)
ʃ-ʃ-ʃ-ʃ-ʃ-ʃ-ʃ-ʃ-ʃ (breath) ʃ-ʃ-ʃ-ʃ-ʃ-ʃ-ʃ-ʃ-ʃ (breath)
ʃ-ʃ-ʃ-ʃ-ʃ-ʃ-ʃ-ʃ-ʃ-ʃ-ʃ (breath) ʃ-ʃ-ʃ-ʃ-ʃ-ʃ-ʃ-ʃ-ʃ-ʃ-ʃ (breath)
ʃ-ʃ-ʃ-ʃ-ʃ-ʃ-ʃ-ʃ-ʃ-ʃ-ʃ-ʃ-ʃ-ʃ-ʃ-ʃ-ʃ (breath)

Keep your focus on the pant, and practice these exercises until the catch breath becomes second nature. Control of the breath is the foundation of all voice work.

Building Breath Capacity

It is always comforting for actors to feel that they have enough breath to sustain a long thought. In general, as long as you are speaking, you will probably have enough breath to get to the end of a long phrase, because while you are speaking the vocal folds (also called the vocal cords) are closed and vibrating. When you pause or stop speaking, the vocal folds open, and you lose the top of the air column and therefore need to breathe again, or "top the tank."

Exercise: **Breath Capacity**

A simple exercise to increase breath capacity is to count from one to twenty and upward, taking a breath on top of the breath you have just taken after each new number. It also helps to lift the last number before the breath in pitch on an upward inflection.

Continue to twenty, and practice daily until you extend your capacity to thirty and beyond without strain. Make sure that you let one word run into the next until you come to the pause.

Example:
One ↗ (breath)
One-**two** ↗ (breath)
One-two-**three** ↗ (breath)
One-two-three-**four** ↗ (breath)
One-two-three-four-**five** ↗ (breath)
One-two-three-four-five-**six** ↗ (breath)
One-two-three-four-five-six-**seven** ↗ (breath)
One-two-three-four-five-six-seven-**eight** ↗ (breath)
One-two-three-four-five-six-seven-eight-**nine** ↗ (breath)
One-two-three-four-five-six-seven-eight-nine-**ten** ↗ (breath)
Continue in increments until you can reach 20, 25, 30, 35.

Exercise: **Slow Exhalation**

Blow out all the air in your lungs.
Sip in air, feeling the ribs expand with the breath.
Release the breath very slowly on *shhhh*—until you feel that you are out of breath.
Continue to release on the *shhhh* until you feel a slight "pull" in the diaphragm.
Release into the pull—the breath will automatically come back in to the lungs.
Repeat 5 times.

Connecting Sound to Breath

The breath should be connected to the sound of the voice without a break between the inhalation and the sound.

Exercise: **Connecting Sound to Breath**

Take a quick breath and blow through your lips with your voice making the sound of a motorboat. Let the sound bubble on your lips feeling the vibrations. Notice that in order to sustain the bubbling sound, you have to sustain the breath.

(Breath) *Bubble-bubble-bubble-bubble*

Now let the voice bubble up the scale ↗ and down the scale ↘:

(Breath and voice moves up) ↗ *Bubble-bubble-bubble-bubble* ↗
(Breath and voice moves down) ↘ *Bubble-bubble-bubble-bubble* ↘

This is one of the easiest and safest voice exercises, because you cannot do it unless you are supporting the sound with your voice. Work to sustain the sound for longer intervals.

Breath Support and Rib Breathing

The human voice operates much like the bagpipes, in which the pressure of the air in the bag vibrates the reed to create the sound. Like the bagpipes, it is the unreleased pressure of the breath in the lungs that vibrates the vocal folds to create the sound of the voice. For the actor, it is the pressure of the unreleased air that supports the voice. One problem many actors have is that they tend to exhale before they begin to speak or at the end of a line. This then leaves the voice without any support, which in turn causes the actor to tense the throat muscles to support the voice and to shout to project to an audience.

Rib breathing involves the last two ribs, which are called *floating ribs* because they are attached only to the spine and not to the sternum. As these ribs open with the breath, the diaphragm lowers, allowing more air into the lungs. In a sense, you are creating a small "tank" of air that you don't use up completely at the end of a phrase; just "top the tank" with each breath and continue speaking.

When you are speaking and come to the end of a phrase, take a quick breath; be sure to hold on to the breath with the lower ribs and don't exhale, just take a catch breath on top of the breath you have already taken. Don't overbreathe: the ribs don't expand beyond the rib cage itself. As you practice this with the text, breath support soon becomes second nature.

Punctuation and Breathing

When focusing on the relationship between breath and punctuation, pay attention to the marks of punctuation in the text as a guide but don't be enslaved by them. Since there is no extant copy of Shakespeare's actual writing, we don't know what his punctuation really was. Most current editions of Shakespeare's plays are only educated guesses, and the First Folio edition, which was published seven years after Shakespeare's death, is helpful but not definitive. Your primary focus is to reveal the meaning of the text and that should be your goal. The following are just some guidelines.

Shakespeare's Punctuation

English punctuation has radically changed in the last four hundred years. Modern punctuation is, or at any rate attempts to be, *grammatical*; the earlier system was mainly *rhetorical*. Some directors use the First Folio exclusively, believing that it is the closest to Shakespeare's original text. There is an argument for and against this decision, but the Folio is also full of errors, omissions, and contradictory spellings. Since contemporary scholarship has provided excellent new editions of the texts based on the latest scholarship, it seems strange to ignore them.

However, for the actor looking at the text and judging when to breathe, here are some areas of punctuation to think about.

Grammatical versus Rhetorical System of Punctuation: The Comma

One result of a grammatical system of punctuation, as contrasted with a rhetorical system, is the use of fewer stops. There was a wider use of the comma in Shakespeare's First Folio edition than there is today, and fewer full stops. We base our punctuation now on structure and grammatical form; the old system was largely guided by meaning.

The following is from the First Folio edition of *Hamlet*, showing the use of **rhetorical** punctuation:

> To be, or not to be, that is the Question:
> Whether 'tis Nobler in the minde to suffer
> The Slings and Arrowes of outragious Fortune,
> Or to take Armes against a Sea of troubles,
> And by opposing end them: to dye: to sleepe
> No more; and by a sleepe, to say we end
> The Heart-ake and the thousand Naturall shockes
> That Flesh is heyre too? 'Tis a consummation
> Devoutly to be wish'd.

Hamlet, 3.1.63–71

Here are some examples from contemporary editions of Shakespeare, showing the **grammatical** approach to punctuation:

> To be, or not to be, that is the question:
> Whether 'tis nobler in the mind to suffer
> The slings and arrows of outrageous fortune,
> Or to take arms against a sea of troubles
> And by opposing end them. To die—to sleep,
> No more; and by a sleep to say we end
> The heart-ache and the thousand natural shocks
> That flesh is heir to: 'tis a consummation
> Devoutly to be wished.

Hamlet, 3.1.56–64 (A. L. Rowse)[2]

To be, or not to be—that is the question:
Whether 'tis nobler in the mind to suffer
The slings and arrows of outrageous fortune
Or to take arms against a sea of troubles
And by opposing end them. To die, to sleep
No more, and by a sleep to say we end
The heartache, and the thousand natural shocks
That flesh is heir to. 'Tis a consummation
Devoutly to be wished.

Hamlet, 3.1.56–64 (Pelican)[3]

Inflection and Breathing

Inflection is the rise or fall of pitch or modulation of the voice that indicates a change in meaning or intention. An upward inflection indicates an unfinished thought:

Comes he here tonight? ↗

A downward inflection indicates a completed thought:

You know right well he does. ↙

This does not mean that the actor should always use an upward inflection unless there is a period, but it is what one does naturally when the spoken thought is unfinished. It is also much easier to catch a breath on an upward inflection, so let the inflection rise before breathing at commas, semicolons, and parenthetical phrases.

ROMEO. What, shall this speech be spoke for our excuse? ↗
    Or shall we on without a apology? ↗
BENVOLIO. The date is out of such prolixity: ↗
    We'll have no Cupid hoodwink'd with a scarf, ↗
    Bearing a Tartar's painted bow of lath, ↗
    Scaring the ladies like a crow-keeper; ↗
    Nor no without-book prologue, faintly spoke
    After the prompter, for our entrance: ↗
    But let them measure us by what they will; ↗
    We'll measure them a measure, and be gone. ↙

Romeo and Juliet, 1.4.1–10

Pauses, Punctuation, and Breath

In verse speaking you earn your pauses, as frequent pauses break the line of thought and slow the production to deadly boredom. Avoid breathing with every comma. Breath fuels the thought and shapes the phrasing. Long sentences equal long thoughts and vice versa. Let a long line of thought continue, using upward inflections until you come to the end of the thought.

The following examples of using the breath in spoken text are taken from *Henry V*, act 3, scene 1. They should be regarded as guidelines, not rules. It is a huge speech. The young king has to rally his soldiers to fight through the city walls or lose the battle. There is a lot of noise, and he has to make himself heard as well as understood. It takes a lot of breath control, not just shouting.

Exercise: **Breathe (catch breath)**

Use a catch breath at a colon, semicolon, exclamation point, dash, or bracket to indicate a parenthetical phrase:

Once more unto the breach, dear friends, once more; (breath)
Or close the wall up with our English dead. (breath)
In peace there's nothing so becomes a man
As modest stillness and humility: (breath)
But when the blast of war blows in our ears, (breath)
Then imitate the action of the tiger; (breath)

Henry V, 3.1.1–6

Exercise: **Don't Breathe**

Don't breathe at commas in the middle of a verse line:

> Stiffen the sinews, summon up the blood, (breath)
>
> *Henry V*, 3.1.7

Or when there is no punctuation in a verse line:

> Disguise fair nature with hard-favour'd rage; (breath)
>
> *Henry V*, 3.1.8

Exercise: **Possibly Breathe**

You might possibly breathe at the end of any verse line regardless of punctuation, unless the line is *enjambed*, which means that the thought is carried over to the following line:

> let the brow o'erwhelm it
> As fearfully as doth a gallèd rock
> O'erhang and jutty his confounded base, (breath)
> Swill'd with the wild and wasteful ocean. (breath)
>
> *Henry V*, 3.1.11–14

Practice Selection for Using the Breath

Now practice the entire selection from *Henry V*. Don't exhale at the beginning of lines; keep the breath under the voice, supporting with your lower ribs.

> Once more unto the breach, dear friends, once more; (breath)
> Or close the wall up with our English dead. (breath)
> In peace there's nothing so becomes a man
> As modest stillness and humility: (breath)
> But when the blast of war blows in our ears,
> Then imitate the action of the tiger; (breath)
> Stiffen the sinews, summon up the blood, (breath)
> Disguise fair nature with hard-favour'd rage; (breath)
> Then lend the eye a terrible aspect; (breath)
> Let pry through the portage of the head
> Like the brass cannon; (breath) let the brow o'erwhelm it
> As fearfully as doth a gallèd rock
> O'erhang and jutty his confounded base, (breath)
> Swill'd with the wild and wasteful ocean. (breath)
>
> *Henry V*, 3.1.1–14

Parenthetical Phrases and Inflection

Some of Shakespeare's speeches consist of long parenthetical phrases. Keep the thought moving with an upward inflection until the thought is finished.

> This land of such dear souls, this dear dear land, ↗ (breath)
> Dear for her reputation through the world, ↗ (breath)
> Is now leased out ↗ (breath), I die pronouncing it, ↗ (breath)
> Like to a tenement or pelting farm: ↓
>
> *Richard II*, 2.1.56–59

I will deliver his challenge by word of mouth; ➚ (breath) set
upon Aguecheek a notable report of valour; ➚ (breath) and
drive the gentleman, ➚ (breath) as I know his youth will aptly
receive it, ➚ (breath) into a most hideous opinion of his rage,
skill, fury and impetuosity. ➘

Twelfth Night, 3.4.186–90

With cunning hast thou filch'd my daughter's heart, ➚ (breath)
Turn'd her obedience, ➚ (breath) which is due to me, ➚ (breath)
To stubborn harshness: ➘

A Midsummer Night's Dream, 1.1.40–42

Breathing on And

When the word *and* occurs at the beginning of the verse line, it is
unstressed, and you can always take a quick breath on it rather than
say the word *and* and then breathe.

> Beshrew me much, Emilia,
> I was, unhandsome warrior as I am,
> Arraigning his unkindness with my soul;
> But now I find I had suborn'd the witness,
> **And** he's indicted falsely.

Othello, 3.4.171–75

Also be sure to take a breath at the end of a rhymed couplet, otherwise the rhythm is thrown off.

> **And** nothing 'gainst Time's scythe can make defence (breath)
> Save breed, to brave him when he takes thee hence.

Sonnet 12, 13–14

Putting Breath, Inflection, and Text Together

If you hold on to your breath with support from your lower ribs, letting your intentions carry you through, you will find that your breath will sustain you. The great English actress Edith Evans reportedly said that in a long sentence you should grasp the final word and pull it toward you.[4] You can only accomplish this if you sustain the breath throughout the line.

> These are the forgeries of jealousy: ↗ (breath)
> And never, since the middle summer's spring,
> Met we on hill, in dale, forest or mead, ↗ (breath)
> By paved fountain or by rushy brook, ↗ (breath)
> Or in the beached margent of the sea,
> To dance our ringlets to the whistling wind, ↗ (breath)
> But with thy brawls thou hast disturb'd our sport. ↓
>
> *A Midsummer Night's Dream*, 2.1.82–88

Note that Titania's speech above, after the first line "These are the forgeries of jealousy," could be spoken on one single breath following Tyrone Guthrie's dictum, but I don't recommend making mechanical breathing exercises out of great speeches. I suspect that Guthrie was trying to focus the actor's attention on the need to sustain the breath through a line of thought without breaking it up into unconnected short phrases, punctuated with breaths taken at random.

For additional practice in putting it all together, try the following:

> IAGO. Patience, I say; ↗ (breath) your mind perhaps may change. ↗ (breath)
> OTHELLO. Never, Iago: ↗ (breath) Like to the Pontic sea,
> Whose icy current and compulsive course
> Ne'er feels retiring ebb, but keeps due on
> To the Propontic and the Hellespont, ↗ (breath)
> Even so my bloody thoughts, with violent pace,
> Shall ne'er look back, ne'er ebb to humble love, ↗ (breath)
> Till that a capable and wide revenge

Swallow them up. ↓ (breath) Now, by yond marble heaven,
   ↗ (breath)
In the due reverence of a sacred vow
I here engage my words. ↓

Othello, 3.3.513–22

All the world's a stage, ↗ (breath)
And all the men and women merely players; ↗ (breath)
They have their exits and their entrances; ↗ (breath)
And one man in his time plays many parts, ↗ (breath)
His acts being seven ages. ↘ (breath) At first the infant,
Mewling and puking in the nurse's arms; ↘ (breath)
Then the whining school-boy, with his satchel
And shining morning face, creeping like snail
Unwillingly to school. ↘ (breath) And then the lover,
Sighing like furnace, with a woeful ballad
Made to his mistress' eyebrow. ↘ (breath) Then a soldier,
Full of strange oaths, and bearded like the pard, ↗ (breath)
Jealous in honour, sudden and quick in quarrel, ↗ (breath)
Seeking the bubble reputation
Even in the cannon's mouth. ↘ (breath) And then the justice,
In fair round belly with good capon lin'd, ↗ (breath)
With eyes severe and beard of formal cut, ↗ (breath)
Full of wise saws and modern instances; ↗ (breath)
And so he plays his part. ↘ (breath) The sixth age shifts
Into the lean and slipper'd pantaloon, ↗ (breath)
With spectacles on nose and pouch on side, ↗ (breath)
His youthful hose, well sav'd, a world too wide
For his shrunk shank; ↗ (breath) and his big manly voice,
Turning again toward childish treble, pipes
And whistles in his sound. ↘ (breath) Last scene of all,
That ends this strange eventful history, ↗ (breath)
Is second childishness and mere oblivion; ↗ (breath)
Sans teeth, sans eyes, sans taste, sans every thing. ↘

As You Like It, 2.7.143–70

Summary

Avoid overbreathing. A comfortable breath, with a slight
expansion in the lower ribs, is much easier to control that
a hyperextended breath that goes up into the chest. When
you take the next breath, always breathe on top of the
breath you already have taken, and don't exhale.

Don't "sigh" out a breath before you speak. When you sigh
on the first word in a line, you have just sighed out your
breath support! Be aware of your habitual speaking pat-
terns to see if you are sighing before you speak.

Connect the breath to the change of ideas in the text.
When you are speaking, even a small pause should be followed by a breath if the voice actually stops. We pause,
and breathe before speaking again, because the thought
has changed—just as we do in life.

> (Breath) Yes, sir, to Milford-Haven; which is the
>   way?—(breath)
> I thank you.—(breath) By yond bush?—(breath) Pray,
>   how far thither? (breath)
> 'Ods pittikins! can it be six mile yet?—(breath)
> I have gone all night. (breath) 'Faith, I'll lie down
>   and sleep.
>
> *Cymbeline*, 4.2.375–78

2

Voice Work for Shakespeare

Shall we clap into't roundly, without hawking, or spitting, or saying we are hoarse, which are the only prologues to a bad voice?
—*As You Like It*, 5.3.9–11

Resonance

Resonance in the human speaking voice is the reinforcement and amplification of spoken sounds in the head, mouth, throat, chest, and lower back of the body. It enables an actor to communicate with an audience in a large space without vocal strain.

The speaking voice, unlike the singing voice, has only one register. The terms *head voice* and *chest voice* as applied to singing would apply only to the chest voice for the speaking voice. This doesn't mean that you don't use the head as a resonator—you do: it is the principal resonator. It's just that singers sometimes get confused when beginning to work on the head and the chest resonators for the speaking voice.

Speaking Shakespeare's text in performance requires vocal virtuosity. The actor must be able to breathe on a quick breath to support the voice, while allowing the resonance of the voice to amplify the sounds of the text, communicating the meaning of the lines, as a character, to an audience.

Optimal Pitch

The optimal pitch of the speaking voice is the baseline pitch found in the middle of the range of the speaking voice. It is determined by many factors, including sex (men's voices are an octave lower than women's voices), the thickness and size of the vocal folds, the bone structure of the face, and other elements that are subtle and hard to pin down. Generally, you can find the optimal pitch of your speaking voice on any voiced consonant. The next chapter, which focuses on diction, will explore the vowels and consonants and how the placement of the lips, tongue, and jaw connects with the work on resonance.

When you begin working with Shakespeare's text, you will become aware of the repeated vowels (assonance) and repeated consonants (alliteration) and how they contribute to the resonance and power of the voice. Speaking Shakespeare's text with focus on the vowels and consonants will enhance the resonance of the voice as well as contribute to the audience's ability to hear and understand the text.

Nasal Resonance

Feel the vibrations on the lips on the consonants *m-n-ŋ*. Each time you intone these consonants, the sound comes through your nose. The nasal consonants are focused forward in the frontal bones of the face where the sounds vibrate. The nasal consonants can move up or down in pitch but don't have the range of the vowels. (A complete chart of the sounds and symbols of the International Phonetic Alphabet appears on page 55.)

m	n	ŋ	
m—ɑː	n—ɑː	ŋ—ɑː	ɑː (ah)
m—oŏ	n—oŏ	ŋ—oŏ	oŏ (oh)
m—uː	n—uː	ŋ—uː	uː (oo)
m—ɔː	n—ɔː	ŋ—ɔː	ɔː (aw)
m—ɜː	n—ɜː	ŋ—ɜː	ɜː (err)

Then sing him home.

Head Resonance and Chest Resonance

The performer's speaking voice is a balance between head resonance and chest resonance. When the voice is focused forward in the "mask" of the face, the chest resonator acts as a woofer, and the head voice acts as the tweeter in much the same way as a stereo. Don't try to push the voice down for more chest resonance—keep the voice focused forward and let the chest resonate normally.

Exercises: **Chest Resonance**

1. Blow through your lips and on to the consonant *m*, dropping the jaw for the vowel *ah*; clasp the palms together and shake the upper torso. Sustain the vowel and let the chest resonate. Work up and down the scale through the middle and lower parts of the voice.

   m–ah–ah–ah–ah–ah

2. Place your hands on your chest. Inhale, then intone *m–ah*, focusing forward in the mask and at the same time feeling the vibration in the chest for the *ah*. Repeat on lower pitches, blending the tone.

   m–ah

Connecting the Resonators

Try to practice your resonance exercises daily until vocal resonance becomes secure and second nature. When working through chapter 3 on articulation of the sounds, remember that the voiced consonants as well as the vowels should be the focus of resonance.

To focus on connecting the resonators, place your hands across your midsection, breathe in, feel the lower ribs expand slightly, and begin to pant. Keep the pant steady and don't push the muscle—let the breath do it.

Exercise: **Connecting the Resonators**

Pant on: *m ... m ... m ... m* (feel the vibrations behind the upper lip).

Drop the jaw and continue the pant on: *ha... ha... ha... ha* (feel the vibrations in the chest).

Move up on pitch, note by note:

m ... m ... m ... m   *ha ... ha ... ha ... ha*   (breath, change note)
m ... m ... m ... m   *ha ... ha ... ha ... ha*   (breath, change note)
m ... m ... m ... m   *ha ... ha ... ha ... ha*   (breath, change note)
m ... m ... m ... m   *ha ... ha ... ha ... ha*   (breath, change note)

Feel the resonance on the sounds. Remember that the nasal consonants come through the nose, and the vowels and other consonant sounds come through the mouth. The "motor" is the solar plexus, or epigastrium.

Practice this exercise without pushing the muscles; just let the breath do the work.

Harmonic Properties in the Speaking Voice

Harmonics are present in the sounds of both the human voice and musical instruments, and they add a lot of richness to the sound of the voice. Without harmonics, the voice would sound thin, flat, and colorless. We normally don't hear the harmonics as separate tones, because they have an increasingly lower amplitude than the fundamental frequency the higher up they go, but they are an essential part of the speaking voice.

One might ask, where do harmonics come from, or more precisely, how are they produced? If you play the guitar, you are probably familiar with harmonics and how to produce them by lightly touching a string, even if you don't fully understand how they work. In the human voice, harmonies are produced by vibrations of the vocal cords amplified by the head and chest resonators.

Exercise: **Harmonic Properties in Resonance**

Hum on the nasal consonant *m-m-m*, then drop the jaw down to the vowel *ah*, sustaining the *m-m-m* into *ah*. Now using the forefinger up and down against the lips, intone the *α:* sound. Notice the harmonic interplay of notes in the sounds. Repeat up and down the scale.

α: (ah) ≈≈≈≈≈ *α:* ≈≈≈≈≈ *α:* ≈≈≈≈≈ *α:* ≈≈≈≈≈

Chanting and Speaking

Chanting is an ancient form of voice production that is still used for religious ceremonies—for example, Gregorian chant. It is half speaking and half singing, or as the Germans call it, *Sprechgesang* (sung speech). Chanting focuses on the middle range of the voice for both men and women. If you are having difficulties with resonance and pitch, chanting is an excellent exercise for bringing the voice forward. It is also helpful in cases of vocal fry, because you have to let the voice move from word to word without a break.

Exercises: **Chanting**

Hum on *m*, feeling the vibrations on the lips on a middle pitch. Then begin to chant this incantation by the witches in *Macbeth*.

FIRST WITCH. Thrice the brinded cat hath **m**ew'd.
SECOND WITCH. Thrice and once the hedge-pig whined.
THIRD WITCH. Harpier cries 'Tis ti**m**e, 'tis ti**m**e.
FIRST WITCH. Round about the cauldron go;
    In the poison'd entrails throw.
    Toad, that under cold stone
    Days and nights has thirty-one
    Swelter'd veno**m** sleeping got,
    Boil thou first i' the char**m**èd pot.

ALL. Double, double toil and trouble;
    Fire burn, and cauldron bubble.
SECOND WITCH. Fillet of a fenny snake,
    In the cauldron boil and bake;
    Eye of newt and toe of frog,
    Wool of bat and tongue of dog,
    Adder's fork and blind-worm's sting,
    Lizard's leg and owlet's wing,
    For a charm of powerful trouble,
    Like a hell-broth boil and bubble.
ALL. Double, double toil and trouble;
    Fire burn and cauldron bubble.
THIRD WITCH. Scale of dragon, tooth of wolf,
    Witches' mummy, maw and gulf
    Of the ravin'd salt-sea shark,
    Root of hemlock digg'd i' the dark,
    Liver of blaspheming Jew,
    Gall of goat, and slips of yew
    Silver'd in the moon's eclipse,
    Nose of Turk and Tartar's lips,
    Finger of birth-strangled babe
    Ditch-deliver'd by a drab,
    Make the gruel thick and slab:
    Add thereto a tiger's chaudron,
    For the ingredients of our cauldron.
ALL. Double, double toil and trouble;
    Fire burn and cauldron bubble.
SECOND WITCH. Cool it with a baboon's blood,
    Then the charm is firm and good.

    . . . .

SECOND WITCH. By the pricking of my thumbs,
    Something wicked this way comes.
    Open, locks,
    Whoever knocks!

Macbeth, 4.1.1–37, 46–49

Here is the lullaby the fairies sing to lull Titania to sleep in *A Midsummer Night's Dream*. Don't push the sound down in your chest or in the throat. Let it come from the lips and vibrate in the front of the face.

> You spotted snakes with double tongue,
> Thorny hedgehogs, be not seen;
> Newts and blind-worms, do no wrong,
> Come not near our fairy queen.
> Philomel, with melody
> Sing in our sweet lullaby;
> Lulla, lulla, lullaby, lulla, lulla, lullaby:
> Never harm,
> Nor spell nor charm,
> Come our lovely lady nigh;
> So, good night, with lullaby.
> Weaving spiders, come not here;
> Hence, you long-legg'd spinners, hence!
> Beetles black, approach not near;
> Worm nor snail, do no offence.
> Philomel, with melody
> Sing in our sweet lullaby;
> Lulla, lulla, lullaby, lulla, lulla, lullaby.
>
> *A Midsummer Night's Dream*, 2.2.10–24

Vocal Music

There are some speeches in Shakespeare that almost seem to have been written to be spoken to music. They are not chanted, but the beauty of the poetry creates a mood for the audience. Here is Oberon from *A Midsummer Night's Dream*:

> I know a bank where the wild thyme blows,
> Where oxlips and the nodding violet grows,
> Quite over-canopied with luscious woodbine,
> With sweet musk-roses and with eglantine:
> There sleeps Titania sometime of the night,

Lull'd in these flowers with dances and delight;
And there the snake throws her enamell'd skin,
Weed wide enough to wrap a fairy in:
And with the juice of this I'll streak her eyes,
And make her full of hateful fantasies.

A Midsummer Night's Dream, 2.1.260–70

In *The Tempes*t the monster Caliban's speech suddenly becomes poetical as he describes the island where he lives:

Be not afeard; the isle is full of noises,
Sounds and sweet airs, that give delight and hurt not.
Sometimes a thousand twangling instruments
Will hum about mine ears, and sometime voices
That, if I then had waked after long sleep,
Will make me sleep again: and then, in dreaming,
The clouds methought would open and show riches
Ready to drop upon me that, when I waked,
I cried to dream again.

The Tempest, 3.2.137–45

In *Cymbeline*, Imogen, disguised as a boy, appears to be dead, and her brother Arviragus speaks these words over her body as they lay her on a bier:

With fairest flowers
Whilst summer lasts and I live here, Fidele,
I'll sweeten thy sad grave: thou shalt not lack
The flower that's like thy face, pale primrose, nor
The azured harebell, like thy veins, no, nor
The leaf of eglantine, whom not to slander,
Out-sweeten'd not thy breath: the ruddock would,
With charitable bill,—O bill, sore-shaming
Those rich-left heirs that let their fathers lie
Without a monument!—bring thee all this;
Yea, and furr'd moss besides, when flowers are none,
To winter-ground thy corse.

Cymbeline, 4.2.290–301

Shouting on Stage

When shouting on stage, be sure to breathe first, then support your breath with your lower ribs. Don't tighten the throat muscles. Place the voice forward in the mask of the face. Be sure to take the catch breath on top of the breath you have already taken.

Some examples that call for shouting:

> FIRST PIRATE. Hold, villain!
> SECOND PIRATE. A prize! a prize!
> THIRD PIRATE. Half-part, mates, half-part.
> Come, let's have her aboard suddenly.
>
> *Pericles*, 4.1.105–8

> Awake, awake!
> Ring the alarum-bell. Murder and treason!
> Banquo and Donalbain! Malcolm! awake!
> Shake off this downy sleep, death's counterfeit,
> And look on death itself! up, up, and see
> The great doom's image! Malcolm! Banquo!
> As from your graves rise up, and walk like sprites,
> To countenance this horror! Ring the bell.
>
> *Macbeth*, 2.3.101–8

> The game's afoot:
> Follow your spirit, and upon this charge
> Cry 'God for Harry, England, and Saint George!'
>
> *Henry V*, 3.1.31–33

Shouting Over Stage Noise

When there is ambient noise on stage, or loud background noise, it is important to pitch the voice slightly higher so that it carries over the background noise without being drowned out by it. Try to get a sense of the general pitch of the sound and then pitch the voice up and over it.

Exercise: **Shouting Over Stage Noise**

The following edited selection from the opening scene of act 1 of *The Tempest* takes place during a terrific storm with thunder, lightning, wind, and the sound of the sea. Make sure you breathe with the lower ribs, hold on to the breath, and articulate, paying special attention to the consonants. Keep the voice forward, and don't push from your throat.

> [*On a ship at sea: a tempestuous noise of thunder and lightning heard.*]
> [*Enter a* MASTER *and a* BOATSWAIN]
> MASTER. Boatswain!
> BOATSWAIN. Here, master: what cheer?
> MASTER. Good, speak to the mariners: fall to't, yarely, or we run ourselves aground: bestir, bestir.
> [*Enter* MARINERS]
> BOATSWAIN. Heigh, my hearts! cheerly, cheerly, my hearts! yare, yare! Take in the topsail. Tend to the master's whistle. Blow, till thou burst thy wind, if room enough!
>
> . . . .
>
> BOATSWAIN. Down with the topmast! yare! lower, lower! Bring her to try with main-course.
> [*A cry within*]
> A plague upon this howling! they are louder than the weather or our office.
>
> . . . .
>
> BOATSWAIN. Lay her a-hold, a-hold! set her two courses off to sea again; lay her off.
> [*Enter* MARINERS *wet, with* ANTONIO, SEBASTIAN, *and* GONZALO]
> MARINERS. All lost! to prayers, to prayers! all lost!
> BOATSWAIN. What, must our mouths be cold?
>
> . . . .

[*A confused noise within: 'Mercy on us!'—'We split, we split!'—
'Farewell, my wife and children!'—'Farewell, brother!'—'We
split, we split, we split!'*]

ANTONIO. Let's all sink with the king.

SEBASTIAN. Let's take leave of him.

[*Exeunt* ANTONIO *and* SEBASTIAN]

GONZALO. Now would I give a thousand furlongs of sea for an
     acre of barren ground, long heath, brown furze, any thing.
     The wills above be done! but I would fain die a dry death.

[*Exeunt*]

The Tempest, 1.1.72–82 (edited)

Stage Whisper

A stage whisper is a loud whisper spoken by an actor on stage that
is meant to be heard by the audience. It is not quite a real whisper;
it's voice overlaid with breath. Bring the voice forward in the mask
of the face, breathe and support with your ribs, and speak in a nor-
mal tone as you exhale slightly, allowing the breath to mix with the
vocal tone.

- Hush! here comes Antony.
- But hush! no more,
- You perceive my mind?
- Mark, how they whisper:
- Good my lord, be quiet.
- No words, no words! hush.

Practice Selections for Stage Whispering

Hush, my gentle neighbours!
Lend me your hands; to the next chamber bear her.
Get linen: now this matter must be look'd to,
For her relapse is mortal. Come, come;
And Aesculapius guide us!

Pericles, 3.2.132–36

Pray you, tread softly, that the blind mole may not
Hear a foot fall: we now are near his cell.

The Tempest, 4.1.237–38

LADY MACBETH. My husband!
MACBETH. I have done the deed. Didst thou not hear a noise?
LADY MACBETH. I heard the owl scream and the crickets cry.
   Did not you speak?
MACBETH. When?
LADY MACBETH. Now.
MACBETH. As I descended?
LADY MACBETH. Ay.
MACBETH. Hark!
   Who lies i' the second chamber?
LADY MACBETH. Donalbain.
MACBETH. This is a sorry sight.
[*Looking on his hands*]
LADY MACBETH. A foolish thought, to say a sorry sight.

Macbeth, 2.2.17–30

Vocal Dynamics

There are speeches in which the vocal dynamics range from an almost-whisper to full volume. In this speech from *The Tempest* in which Prospero gives up his magical powers, he first summons the fairies whose power is entwined with his, and as he does so, his power slowly builds until he has broken his staff and given up his power.

Ye elves of hills, brooks, standing lakes and groves, (breath)
And ye that on the sands with printless foot
Do chase the ebbing Neptune and do fly him
When he comes back; (breath) you demi-puppets that
By moonshine do the green sour ringlets make,
Whereof the ewe not bites, (breath) and you whose pastime
Is to make midnight mushrooms, that rejoice
To hear the solemn curfew; (breath) by whose aid, (breath)
Weak masters though ye be, (breath) I have bedimm'd
The noontide sun, call'd forth the mutinous winds, (breath)
And 'twixt the green sea and the azured vault
Set roaring war: (breath) to the dread rattling thunder
Have I given fire and rifted Jove's stout oak
With his own bolt; (breath) the strong-based promontory
Have I made shake and by the spurs pluck'd up
The pine and cedar: (breath) graves at my command
Have waked their sleepers, oped, and let 'em forth
By my so potent art. (breath) But this rough magic
I here abjure, (breath) and, when I have required
Some heavenly music, which even now I do, (breath)
To work mine end upon their senses that
This airy charm is for, I'll break my staff, (breath)
Bury it certain fathoms in the earth, (breath)
And deeper than did ever plummet sound
I'll drown my book.

The Tempest, 5.1.38–62

3

The Sounds of English in Shakespeare's Text

Speaking Shakespeare's text requires a control of spoken English. The ability to manage the sounds of the English language, to speak quickly without garbling the lines, to articulate complex sentence structures while conveying the meaning of what is being said, is the hallmark of the trained Shakespearean actor and requires a mastery of the sounds of the English language. Perhaps the best advice given to actors about speaking Shakespeare's language comes from Shakespeare himself in Hamlet's advice to the players:

> Speak the speech, I pray you, as I pronounc'd it to you, trippingly on the tongue. But if you mouth it, as many of our players do, I had as live the town crier spoke my lines. Nor do not saw the air too much with your hand, thus, but use all gently; for in the very torrent, tempest, and (as I may say) whirlwind of your passion, you must acquire and beget a temperance that may give it smoothness. O, it offends me to the soul to hear a robustious periwig-pated fellow tear a passion to tatters, to very rags, to split the ears of the groundlings, who (for the most part) are capable of nothing but inexplicable dumb shows and noise. I would have such a fellow whipp'd for o'erdoing Termagant. It out-herods Herod. Pray you avoid it . . . Be not too tame neither; but let your own discretion be your tutor. Suit the action to the word, the word to the action; with this special

observance, that you o'erstep not the modesty of nature: for anything so overdone is from the purpose of playing, whose end, both at the first and now, was and is, to hold, as 'twere, the mirror up to nature; to show Virtue her own feature, scorn her own image, and the very age and body of the time his form and pressure. Now this overdone, or come tardy off, though it make the unskilful laugh, cannot but make the judicious grieve; the censure of the which one must in your allowance o'erweigh a whole theatre of others.

Hamlet, 3.2.1–29

The sounds of a language are the building blocks that make up the words by which we communicate. Actors in all languages are expected to be masters of the sounds of their own language.

This chapter will introduce all the consonants, vowels, and diphthongs of the English language and will focus on specific diction challenges that occur in Shakespeare's text, illustrated with selections from his plays. In the English-speaking theater, we are fortunate that one of our greatest poets is also our greatest dramatist. All the sounds in English will be shown using the International Phonetic Alphabet (IPA).

The International Phonetic Alphabet

The International Phonetic Alphabet (IPA) is a series of symbols, based primarily on Latin, which serves as a standardized representation of the sounds of oral language. It is used by foreign-language students, teachers, speech-language pathologists, actors, singers, linguists, and anyone trying to identify the exact nature of the sounds of English.

Why Do We Use the International Phonetic Alphabet?

English is a decidedly unphonetic language. This means that the spelling of a word, more often than not, has no relation to the pronunciation of the word.

The following words are homonyms, which are words that sound the same but mean different things and may have different spellings. These homonyms are spelled differently:

ri:d
_____

reed

> I had as lief have a **reed** that will do
> me no service as a partisan I could not heave.
> > *Anthony and Cleopatra*, 2.7.10–11

read

> Nay, I'll **read** it first, by your favour.
> > *All's Well That Ends Well*, 4.3.207

rede

> Himself the primrose path of dalliance treads
> And recks not his own **rede**.
> > *Hamlet*, 1.3.52–53

These next homonyms are spelled and pronounced the same, but again, the meaning is different:

laĭ
_____

lie

> I had rather **lie** in the woolen.
> > *Much Ado about Nothing*, 2.1.24

> Should I **lie**, madam?
> > *Antony and Cleopatra*, 2.5.124

And here again, the sound is the same, but the spellings and the meanings are different:

soʊlz

*soles/soul/***sole**

> MERCUTIO. Nay, gentle Romeo, we must have you dance.
> ROMEO. Not I, believe me: you have dancing shoes
>   With nimble **soles**: I have a **soul** of lead
>   So stakes me to the ground I cannot move.
> > *Romeo and Juliet*, 1.4.12–15

> Is she **sole** child to the king?
> > *Cymbeline*, 1.1.56

Since the sounds of the words are alike, the actor should take note of them. These homonyms are part of the word play that the character uses to communicate what he or she is thinking and feeling to the other characters.

For instance, in the opening lines of *Richard III*, Richard, Duke of Gloucester, uses the word *son* to point up the fact that his brother, Edward IV, whose symbol in heraldry was the sun, is now king. That is implied by the homonym *son/sun* (sʌn):

> Now is the winter of our discontent
> Made glorious summer by this **son** of York;
> > *Richard III*, 1.1.1–2

The Makeup of the International Phonetic Alphabet

> Let us make the fullest possible use of the International Phonetic Alphabet as an auxiliary, both in our schools and in our classes for foreigners; if we wish to show what the phonemes in English are, here at least is a scientific way of doing so.
> > Anthony Burgess[1]

There are 26 letters in the English alphabet and 48 sounds in the English language, with many words spelled differently but with the same pronunciation. Although at first the IPA may seem cumbersome, it is a basic system of indicating sounds of spoken language regardless of the spelling. It is used in the worlds of both opera and theater. The IPA is a tool that you will easily become familiar with. It always gives the correct symbol for the sound despite the spelling.

International Phonetic Alphabet

The English Vowels and Diphthongs

iː	ɪ	ɪɚ	e	ɛɚ	eɪ	æ	a	aɪ
ease	it	ear	end	air	aid	apple	ask	aye

ɜː	ə	ʌ
irk	a	up

uː	ʊ	ʊɚ	o	oʊ	ɔː	ɔɪ	ɔɚ	ɒ	ɑː	ɑʊ	ɑɚ
who	pull	ewer	obey	oh	awe	oil	oar	honor	alms	our	art

The English Consonants

p - b	t - d	k - g
pop bob	tot did	gig coke

m - n - ŋ
hum nun hung

f - v	θ - ð	s - z	ʃ - ʒ	r - h
fife viva	thigh thy	sue zoo	shy azure	red h

tʃ - dʒ
chew Jew

ʍ - w	j
whit wit	you

The English Consonants

Consonants are the structural framework of the English language, which is Germanic and derived from the consonant-based Anglo-Saxon that supplanted the Gaelic spoken by the early Britons. Anglo-Saxon evolved into Old English, then into Middle English, and finally into the Early Modern English which Shakespeare wrote.

The consonants of English anchor the text, and Shakespeare makes use of their acoustic, alliterative, and rhythmical properties in all his plays. When practicing the consonants, be aware of how the sounds focus the voice.

Consonants and Alliteration

The alliterative rhythm of the consonants occurs not only in Modern English but can also be heard in this translation of *Beowulf* from the Anglo-Saxon.

> Lo, **pr**aise of the **pr**owess of **p**eople-kings
> of **sp**ear-armed **D**anes, in **d**ays long sped,
> we **h**ave **h**eard, and what **h**onor the athelings won!
> Oft **Sc**yld the **Sc**efing from **s**quadroned foes,
> from **m**any a tribe, the **m**ead-bench tore,
> awing the **e**arls. Since **e**rst he lay
> **fr**iendless, a **f**oundling, **f**ate repaid him:
> for he **w**axed under **w**elkin, in **w**ealth he throve,
> till be**f**ore him the **f**olk, both **f**ar and near,
> who **h**ouse by the **wh**ale-path, **h**eard his mandate,
> **g**ave him **g**ifts: a **g**ood king he!
>
> *Beowulf*[2]

Shakespeare, writing in Early Modern English, certainly used alliteration frequently in his plays, to especially comic effect in the Rude Mechanicals' performance of *Pyramus and Thisbe* in *A Midsummer Night's Dream*:

> Whereat, with **bl**ade, with **bl**oody **bl**ameful **bl**ade,
> He **br**avely **br**oach'd his **b**oiling **bl**oody **br**east;
>
> *A Midsummer Night's Dream*, 5.1.159–60

Or to create the somber mood in the opening of *Romeo and Juliet*:

> From **f**orth the **f**atal loins of these two **f**oes
> A **p**air of star-cross'd lovers take their li**f**e;
> Whose misadventured **p**iteous overthows
> **D**o with their **d**eath bury their **p**arent's strife.
> *Romeo and Juliet*, prologue.5–8

The alliteration of repeated consonants also drives the rhythm of the text, and all work with consonants should include specific attention to the alliterative qualities and effects of Shakespeare's writing.

The Nasal Consonants: m, n, ŋ

The nasal consonants are the only sounds in English that resonate through the nose. The nasal consonants give richness and timbre to the voice and help give it focus.

Sometimes actors avoid the nasal consonants in the mistaken idea that they will make the voice sound nasal. In fact, what actors usually think of as nasality is just its opposite, denasalization, a condition that sounds like a perpetual head cold. The vibration of the nasal consonants helps the voice carry and supports the text.

As you make the following sounds, you should feel the vibration where sound is made on all nasal consonants:

m—both lips

> To play with **m**ammets . . .
> *Henry IV, Part 1*, 2.3.92

n—tip of the tongue on gum ridge

> I'll **n**one now:
> *Antony and Cleopatra*, 2.5.11

ŋ—back of the tongue on soft palate

> I am sure ha**ng**ing's the way of winki**ng**.
> *Cymbeline*, 5.4.209

Now hum, allowing your voice to switch from nasal to oral resonators on the three nasal consonants:

hʌm—ɑː
hʌn—ɑː
hʌŋ—ɑː

Practice the following exercises for resonance on the nasal consonants. Start on a middle pitch and go up and down the scale, letting
the voice switch easily from the nasal resonator to the oral resonator:

hʌm—ɑː—ɔː—oʊ—uː—iː
hʌn—ɑː—ɔː—oʊ—uː—iː
hʌŋ—ɑː—ɔː—oʊ—uː—iː

Don't nasalize the vowel æ when m/n/ŋ follows the sound:

m	*n*	*ŋ*
lamb	land	languish
stammer	stand	stank
sam	sand	sang
dam	dandle	dangle
gamble	gander	gangle
hammer	handle	hang
clam	clan	clank

Alliteration with Nasal Consonants *m, n, ŋ*
The nasal consonants within the following phrases give extra reso-
nance and help the actors communicate the meaning to the audience.
- rave**n**ing first the la**mb**
- Trust **n**ot to rotte**n** pla**n**ks
- About her la**n**k and all o'erteemèd loi**n**s,
- For **m**ischiefs **m**anifold
- she vaunted '**m**ongst her **m**inions
- Thou ca**n**st **n**ot vex **m**e with i**n**constant **m**ind

Chant the following lines spoken by the witches in *Macbeth*. Feel the resonance on the nasal consonants. Repeat, catching a breath at the end of *come*, letting the voice move up and down in pitch. Don't stop the voice between the words; let one run into the other:

> A drum, a drum!
> Macbeth doth come. (breath)
> A drum, a drum!
> Macbeth doth come. (breath)
> A drum, a drum!
> Macbeth doth come.
>
> *Macbeth*, 1.3.31–32

Practice Selections for *m, n, ŋ*

Note the nasal consonants and practice speaking the following excerpts, placing particular emphasis on letting the resonance work to communicate the meaning:

> By the pricking of my thumbs,
> Something wicked this way comes.
> Open, locks,
> whoever knocks!
>
> *Macbeth*, 4.1.46–49

> In God's name and the king's, say who thou art
> And why thou comest thus knightly clad in arms,
> Against what man thou comest, and what thy quarrel:
> Speak truly, on thy knighthood and thy oath;
> As so defend thee heaven and thy valour!
>
> *Richard II*, 1.3.14–18

> Then the whining school-boy, with his satchel
> And shining morning face, creeping like snail
> Unwillingly to school.
>
> *As You Like It*, 2.7.149–51

The Stop Plosives: **p-b, t-d, k-g**

In Shakespeare's text, the stop plosives are percussive, and the alliteration of the repeated plosives creates a rhythm that drives the text. This applies to both Shakespeare's verse and his prose.

The stop-plosive consonants *p/t/k* are voiceless, while *b/d/g* are voiced.

p-b—made with the lips
- The **p**a**p** of **P**yramus;
- **B**eaten, **b**adly **b**eaten,

t-d—made with the tip of the tongue
- ou**t**, **t**awny **T**artar, ou**t**!
- **D**ainty **d**uck! O **d**ear!

k-g—made with the back of the tongue
- **K**ate of my **c**onsolation;
- **G**od's **g**oodness hast been **g**reat to thee

In addition, the voiceless stop-plosive consonants in English are either *aspirated* or *unaspirated*. If *aspirated*, they are released before a vowel or a pause:

p^h—t^h—k^h
- I **p**ray you, **t**arry; **p**ause a day or two,
- if thou **t**ak'st leave, thou wert better be hang'd
- Your cuc**k**oo sings by kind.

If *unaspirated*, they are held but not released before another consonant:

p₁—t₁—k₁
- They have o'erlook'd me, and divided me
- And sends them weapons wra**pp**ed about with lines,
- Which I shall send you wri**tt**en, be assured,

These are general rules for quickly spoken speech. An actor can decide to release both plosives for a strong effect:

> Macduff was from his mother's womb
> Untimely ri**pp'd**.
>
> *Macbeth*, 5.8.19–20

> From Cupid's shoulder **p**luck his **p**ainted wings
> And fly with me **t**o Cressid!
>
> *Troilus and Cressida*, 3.2.14–15

> S**p**eak the s**p**eech, I **p**ray you, as I **p**ronounc'd it to you, tri**p-p**ingly on the tongue. But if you mouth it, as many of your **p**layers do, I had as live the town crier s**p**oke my lines.
>
> *Hamlet*, 3.2.1–3

Alliteration with Stop Plosives
- **P**rithee **P**etruchio **p**erchance your **p**rattling **p**rey is from **P**adua **p**arted.
- **D**ead for a **d**ucat, **d**ead!
- But s**c**rew your **c**ourage to the sti**ck**ing place, and we'll not fail.
- **D**ear heart, for**b**ear to **g**lance thine eye asi**d**e.
- They'll su**ck** our **b**reath, or **p**inch us **bl**ack and blue.
- You **d**raw me, you har**d**-hear**t**ed a**d**amant

Practice Selections for Stop Plosives

. . . he cannot 'scape me; 'tis impossible he should; he cannot creep into a halfpenny purse, nor into a pepper-box: but, lest the devil that guides him should aid him, I will search impossible places.

The Merry Wives of Windsor, 3.5.135–39

Yet I,
A dull and muddy-mettled rascal, peak
Like John-a-dreams, unpregnant of my cause,
And can say nothing! No, not for a king,
Upon whose property and most dear life
A damn'd defeat was made.

Hamlet, 2.2.556–61

Bell, book, and candle shall not drive me back,
When gold and silver becks me to come on.

King John, 3.3.13–14

Ring the alarum bell! Blow, wind! come, wrack!
At least we'll die with harness on our back.

Macbeth, 5.5.59–60

Pray the gods to intermit the plague
That needs must light on this ingratitude.

Julius Caesar, 1.1.54–55

You lie, in faith, for you are call'd plain Kate,
And bonny Kate, and sometimes Kate the curst;
But, Kate, the prettiest Kate in Christendom,
Kate of Kate Hall, my super-dainty Kate,
For dainties are all Kates, and therefore, Kate,
Take this of me, Kate of my consolation–
Hearing thy mildness prais'd in every town,
Thy virtues spoke of, and thy beauty sounded,
Yet not so deeply as to thee belongs,
Myself am mov'd to woo thee for my wife.

The Taming of the Shrew, 2.1.194–203

The Lateral Consonant l

The consonant *l* is produced with the tip of the tongue touching the upper gum ridge, releasing the sound over the sides of the tongue. Don't let the tongue protrude over the upper front teeth or pull back in the throat. Feel the vibrations on the tip of the tongue.

> la, la, la / la, la, la
> loo, loo, loo / loo, loo, loo
> lie, lie, lie / lie, lie, lie
> law, law, law / law, law, law
> low, low, low / low, low, low
> lay, lay, lay / lay, lay, lay
> lee, lee, lee / lee, lee, lee
> lurk, lurk, lurk / lurk, lurk, lurk

Intone *l* without allowing the tip of the tongue to push forward or to pull back.

> lily—lily—lily . . . l-l-l-l-l
> lily—lully—lily—lully . . . l-l-l-l-l

Alliteration with *l*

The consonant *l* gives a light liquid sound.
- "Little" again? nothing but "low" and "little"
- lady smocks all silver-white
- lulling on a lewd-love bed

With love's light wings did I o'er perch these walls;
For stony limits cannot hold love out,
And what love can do that dares love attempt;
Therefore thy kinsmen are no let to me.

Romeo and Juliet, 2.2.70–73

'Tis a commodity will lose the gloss with lying; the longer kept,
the less worth:

All's Well That Ends Well, 1.1.153–54

Why rather, sleep, liest thou in smoky cribs,
Upon uneasy pallets stretching thee,
And hush'd with buzzing night-flies to thy slumber,

Richard II, 3.1.8–10

The Fricative Consonants: f-v, θ-ð, s-z, ʃ-ʒ, r, h

Fricative consonants are caused by the release of air or vibration
between two articulators.

f

Release the breath between the lower lip and the upper front teeth.

fee, fie, foe, fair
waft, drift, lift
half, hoof, leaf

Alliteration with *f*
- The thane of **f**i**f**e had a wi**f**e
- **f**ierce **f**iery warriors **f**ought upon the clouds
- This is the **f**oul **f**iend **f**libbertigibbet

Practice Selections for *f*

O fortune, fortune! all men call thee fickle:
If thou art fickle, what dost thou with him.
That is renown'd for faith? Be fickle, fortune;
For then, I hope, thou wilt not keep him long,
But send him back.

Romeo and Juliet, 3.5.67–71

A fool, a fool! I met a fool i' th' forest,
A motley fool. A miserable world!
As I do live by food, I met a fool,
Who laid him down and bask'd him in the sun,
And rail'd on Lady Fortune in good terms,
In good set terms- and yet a motley fool.

As You Like It, 2.7.10–15

Is this the fine of his fines, and the recovery of his recoveries,
to have his fine pate full of fine dirt? Will his vouchers vouch
him no more of his purchases, and double ones too, than the
length and breadth of a pair of indentures?

Hamlet, 5.1.98–102

---

v

Release the vibration of the voice between the lower lip and the
upper front teeth.

> verve, vivid, verily
> level, loved, resolved
> have, grave, move

Alliteration with *v*
- Are you all resolved to give your voices?
- A votary; I have vowed to Jaquenetta to hold the plough
- For canker vice the sweetest buds doth love,

Most sweet **v**oices!
Better it is to die, better to star**v**e,
Than crave the hire which first we do deser**v**e.
Why in this wool**v**ish toge should I stand here,
To beg of Hob and Dick, that do appear,
Their needless **v**ouches?

Coriolanus, 2.3.120–25

Who are the **v**otaries, my loving lords,
That are **v**ow-fellows with this **v**irtuous duke?

Love's Labour's Lost, 2.1.36–37

Virginity being blown down, man will quicklier be blown up:
marry, in blowing him down again, with the breach yoursel**v**es
made, you lose your city. It is not politic in the commonwealth
of nature to preser**v**e **v**irginity. Loss of **v**irginity is rational
increase and there was ne**v**er **v**irgin got till **v**irginity was first
lost. That you were made of is metal to make **v**irgins. **V**irginity
by being once lost may be ten times found; by being ever kept,
it is ever lost: 'tis too cold a companion; away with 't!

All's Well That Ends Well, 1.1.126–35

θ

Release the breath between the front of the tongue and the upper front teeth.

think, thought, theme
anthology, deathlike
forth, doth, myth

Alliteration with *θ*

- The lion dying **th**ruste**th** for**th** his paw
- Why, **th**en, **th**ree-far**th**ing wor**th** of silk.
- **Th**rough A**th**ens I am **th**ought as fair as she.

Practice Selections for *θ*

Some say the lark makes sweet division;
This do**th** not so, for she divide**th** us:
Some say the lark and loa**th**ed toad change eyes,
O, now I would they had changed voices too!

Romeo and Juliet, 3.5.128–31

Thrice to **th**ine, and **th**rice to mine
And **th**rice again, to make up nine.
Peace! the charm's wound up.

Macbeth, 1.3.36–38

Why tell you me of moderation?
The grief is fine, full, perfect, that I taste,
And violente**th** in a sense a strong
As that which cause**th** it:

Troilus and Cressida, 4.4.2–5

ð

The *ð* is the voiced cognate of *θ*. Feel the vibration with the front of
the tongue against the upper front teeth.

this, that, these, those
breathes, bathed, teethes
loathe, seethe, clothe

Alliteration with *ð*

- **Th**ou shalt get kings, **th**ough **th**ou be none:
- And **th**at **th**y tongue some say of breeding brea**th**es,
- Which nature loa**th**es—take **th**ou **th**e destined ten**th**,

Consonant Combinations with ð

This sound requires sustained breath and voicing. Practice the final endings for the following words, making sure not to drop the final voiced consonants:

- close—clothes—closed
- breathes—breeze—breathed
- sheathe—she's—sheathed
- bathe—bays—bathed
- lathe—lays—laid
- tithe—ties—tied
- swathe—sways—swayed
- writhe—rise—writhed
- with—wizard—withered

Practice Selections for ð

Brav'd in mine own house with a skein of thread!
Away, thou rag, thou quantity, thou remnant;
Or I shall so bemete thee with thy yard
As thou shalt think on prating whilst thou liv'st!
I tell thee, I, that thou hast marr'd her gown.
                    The Taming of the Shrew, 4.3.117–21

Be thou blest, Bertram, and succeed thy father
In manners, as in shape! thy blood and virtue
Contend for empire in thee, and thy goodness
Share with thy birthright!
                    All's Well That Ends Well, 1.1.58–61

At 'closes in **the** consequence'—Ay, marry!
He closes **thus**: 'I know the gentleman.
I saw him yesterday, or t'other day,
Or **then**, or **then**, wi**th** such or such; and, as you say,
There was 'a gaming; **th**ere o'ertook in's rouse;
There falling out at tennis'; or perchance,
'I saw him enter such a house of sale,'
Videlicet, a bro**th**el, or so forth.

Hamlet, 2.1.58–65

S-Z

The consonants *s-z* are made with the teeth close together and in line, but not touching. The sides of the tongue touch and hold on to the upper molars, and the tip of the tongue is free and pointing toward the front of the upper gums. The breath is directed in a thin stream against the hard surface of the upper teeth.

so, sue, say	zoo, zero, zeal
beast, castle, burst	bruised, seized, amazed
pass, miss, lass	sighs, muse, flows

Rules for Final *s-z* Sounds in English
There is sometimes confusion in the use of the consonant *s* instead of *z* at end of a word. In English, when a word ends in a voiceless consonant and is either plural or possessive, the *s* is voiceless.

rips	leaf's	writs
tooth's	bakes	myths
mats	hats	cracks

When a word ends in a voiced consonant or a vowel, the *s* is pronounced *z*.

ribs	rids	bags
homes	sins	hangs
wills	lives	breathes
bees	loses	amazes
kisses	awes	breezes

Note that not all words that end with a written vowel cause the final *s* to be pronounced as a *z*. If the vowel is silent (like in *hope*), the *s* is voiceless.

jokes	hopes	hates

Alliteration with *s*
- In sooth I know not why I am so sad.
- sweets with sweets war not, joy delights in joy
- When sorrows come, they come not single spies

Consonant Combinations with *str*
Drag the tip of the tongue from the *t* position at the center of the gum ridge back until it leaves the gum ridge for *r*.

strike	strew	strive	strong	stream
streak	strife	strip	strand	straw
strap	structure	strum	stroke	street
strained	strait	strange	stray	strangle
stretched	strongly	strossers	strumpet	striker

Some examples with *str*:
- **str**ive to mend
- **str**icken **str**ucture
- your **str**ait **str**ossers

Practice Selections for *str*

The quality of mercy is not **str**ain'd,

Merchant of Venice, 4.1.194

O day and night, but this is wondrous **str**ange!

Hamlet, 1.5.184

Thou wrong'st thyself, if thou shouldst **str**ive to choose.

All's Well That Ends Well, 2.3.157

Consonant Combinations with *sts*

Let the final *s* come out of the *t*, which is unaspirated.

- with a mode**st smile**
- That the fi**xed** sentinels
- such **bursts** of horrid thunder

Practice Selections for *sts*

They may break his foaming courser's back,
And throw the rider headlong in the li**sts**,

Richard II, 1.2.49–50

Amen. A man may, if he were of a fearful heart, stagger in this attempt; for here we have no temple but the wood, no assembly but horn-bea**sts**.

As You Like It, 3.3.36–38

My conscience, thou art fetter'd
More than my shanks and wri**sts**: you good gods, give me
The penitent instrument to pick that bolt,
Then, free for ever!

Cymbeline, 5.4.9–12

Contractions and Possessives with *S*

Don't add an extra syllable in a contraction.

- **say'st** thou so
- How oft, when thou, my music, music **play'st**
- Thou **want'st** a rough pash and the shoots that I have,

If a word ends in an *s* and is possessive, don't add an extra *s*.

- Think on me that am with **Phoebus'** amorous pinches black,
- Made to his **mistress'** eyebrow.
- Come, **Cassius'** sword, and find **Titinius'** heart.

Alliteration with *z*

The *z* sound is always voiced and made in the same position as *s*.

- to see my **ewes graze** and my **lambs** suck.
- Your presence **needs** must **puzzle** Antony;
- 'Tribunes!' 'Patricians!' 'Citizens!' 'What, ho!'

Practice Selections for *z*

                              for apes and **monkeys**
'Twixt two such shes would chatter this way and
Contemn with **mows** the other;

Cymbeline, 1.6.43–45

                              but it **is** I
That, lying by the violet in the sun,
Do as the carrion does, not as the flower,
Corrupt with **virtuous** season. Can it be
That modesty may more betray our sense
Than woman's lightness?

Measure for Measure, 2.2.207–13

The hum of either army stilly **sounds**,
That the fixed **sentinels** almost receive
The secret **whispers** of each other's watch:

Henry V, prologue.5–7

The tip of the tongue is pointing up toward the middle of the gum ridge.

> **Sh**oe, **sh**ame, **sh**ine
> wi**sh**ed, hu**sh**ed, ma**sh**ed
> di**sh**, la**sh**, har**sh**

Alliteration with ʃ
- For his **sh**runk **sh**ank,
- Thereby **sh**all we **sh**adow
- And **sh**ivering **sh**ocks

Practice Selections for ʃ

> Nature would not invest herself in such **sh**adowing passion without some instruction. It is not words that **sh**ake me thus. Pish! Noses, ears, and lips.
>
> *Othello*, 4.1.48–50

> It is the lark that sings so out of tune,
> Straining har**sh** discords and unpleasing **sh**arps.
>
> *Romeo and Juliet*, 3.5.26–27

> Thou **sh**ow'dst a subject's **sh**ine . . .
>
> *Pericles*, 1.2.133

This sound comes from the French language, and there are no English words that begin with it. The names Jacques, Genevieve, Jean, and Roget are all French. The sound is made with the tip of the tongue pointing toward the middle of the gum ridge and the sides of the tongue on the back molars.

azure, seizure, vision
leisure, rouge, beige

Alliteration with ʒ

- I wait upon his pleasure
- a good persuasion
- Measure my strangeness with my unripe years:

Practice Selections for ʒ

Peace, ho! I bar confusion;
'Tis I must make conclusion
Of these most strange events.

As You Like It, 5.4.116–18

Haste still pays haste, and leisure answers leisure;
Like doth quit like, and MEASURE still FOR MEASURE.

Measure for Measure, 5.1.449–50

When they next wake, all this derision
Shall seem a dream and fruitless vision,

Midsummer Night's Dream, 3.2.398–99

The consonant *r* is made with the tip of the tongue free and pointing toward the back of the upper gum ridge. The sides of the tongue are touching the back molars and the voice seems to be vibrating just behind the hard palate. Don't let the lips form the *r* sound, as a common problem occurs when the sound is made with the lips rather than with the tip of the tongue. An exaggerated form of this problem would make the phrase *red river* sound like *wed wiver*.

> rue, row, ride
> worry, sorrow, carry

Linguists think that in Shakespeare's time all *r* sounds were strongly pronounced, much as they are in Irish or Scottish today. However, in both British RP and in American English the consonant *r* is pronounced in the strong initial position only if it is followed by a vowel or a diphthong, either in the same word or in the following word. In British English the *r* is dropped before a consonant, and in American English the *r* can be either colored with a slight inflection or pronounced with a slight upward motion of the tongue.

Alliteration with *r*
- **r**uinous **r**oof to **r**uinate
- victo**r**ious **wr**eaths
- Of colour like the **red r**ose on **tr**iumphant briar,

Linking *r*
When a word ends in the letter *r* and the following word begins with a vowel, be sure to link the *r* sound into the vowel.
- He**r** eye discourses, I will answe**r** it
- He's he**r**e in double trust
- make us ado**r**e ou**r** errors

Consonant Combinations with *tr* and *dr*
Don't release the tip of the tongue; instead drag it back for the *r*.
- **tr**ip, Au**dr**ey, **tr**ip
- my thoughts can not **tr**anspose
- Gives his potent regiment to a **tr**ull

- I will **dr**ain him **dry** as hay
- your sister's **dr**own'd, Laertes.
- his **dr**ead trident shake

Practice Selections for *r*

Thus, in this st**r**ange and sad habiliment,
I will encounte**r** with And**r**onicus,
And say I am **R**evenge, sent f**r**om below
To join with him and **r**ight his heinous w**r**ongs.
Knock at his study, whe**r**e, they say, he keeps,
To **r**uminate st**r**ange plots of di**r**e **r**evenge;
Tell him **R**evenge is come to join with him,
And wo**r**k confusion on his enemies.

Titus Andronicus, 5.2.1–12

Go thou and seek the c**r**owner, and let him sit o' my coz; for
he's in the thi**r**d degree of d**r**ink; he's d**r**owned:

Twelfth Night, 1.5.129–31

The g**r**ey-eyed mo**r**n smiles on the f**r**owning night,
Chequering the easte**r**n clouds with st**r**eaks of light,
And flecked darkness like a d**r**unkard **r**eels
From forth day's path and Titan's fiery wheels:

Romeo and Juliet, 2.3.1–4

h

The *h* sound is just a puff of air released over the back of the tongue.
Don't drop this sound in phrases. No words in English end in a spoken *h* sound.

home, here, hail
behold, ahead, unhair

Alliteration with *h*

- Now join your **h**ands, and with your **h**ands your **h**earts.
- Three things that women **h**ighly **h**old in **h**ate.
- My **h**usband **h**ies **h**im **h**ome;

Practice Selections for *h*

To let a fellow that will take rewards
And say 'God quit you!' be familiar with
My playfellow, your **h**and; this kingly seal
And plighter of **h**igh **h**earts! O, that I were
Upon the **h**ill of Basan, to outroar
The **h**orned **h**erd! for I **h**ave savage cause;
And to proclaim it civilly, were like
A **h**alter'd neck which does the **h**angman thank
For being yare about him.

Antony and Cleopatra, 3.13.160–68

For ere Demetrius look'd on **H**ermia's eyne,
He **h**ail'd down oaths that **h**e was only mine;
And when this **h**ail some **h**eat from **H**ermia felt,
So **h**e dissolved, and showers of oaths did melt.
I will go tell **h**im of fair **H**ermia's flight:

A Midsummer Night's Dream, 1.1.253–57

What say you? **H**ence,
Horrible villain! or I'll spurn thine eyes
Like balls before me; I'll un**h**air thy **h**ead:
Thou shalt be whipp'd with wire, and stew'd in brine,
Smarting in lingering pickle.

Antony and Cleopatra, 2.5.80–84

The Glides: ʍ-w, j

The glides are consonants that are almost like vowels in that they begin in a vowel position and then "glide" into the sound.

ʍ-w

In Shakespeare's time, the differences between ʍ and w were clearly distinguished, and they are still pronounced differently in Ireland, Scotland, parts of Northern England, and part of the United States. It's one of the ways in which Shakespeare's English is closer to American English.

The glides ʍ-w begin with the lips in a rounded position for u: (*oo*). For w, round your lips and begin the *oo* sound for w, as in *wear*. It is voiced.

> we, one, want
> aware, acquaint, acquired

For ʍ, round your lips for u: (*oo*) and blow through your lips for *wh*, as in *where*. It is voiceless.

> whet, whence, whither, awhile

Use the following pairs of words to practice the difference between ʍ and w.

white—wight	when—wen	where—wear
whine—wine	while—wile	which—witch
whet—wet	whither—wither	whit—wit
weal—wheel	whether—weather	why—Y

Alliteration with ʍ-w
- Then will two at once woo one;
- which I held my duty speedily to acquaint you withal;
- No, not a whit. What! I have watched ere now

Practice Selections for ʍ-w

A man that had a wife with such a wit, he might say, 'Wit,
whither wilt?'

As You Like It, 4.1.137

Who, every word by all my wit being scann'd,
Want wit in all one word to understand.

The Comedy of Errors, 2.2.146–47

This whimpled, whining, purblind, wayward boy;
This senior-junior, giant-dwarf, Dan Cupid;

Love's Labour's Lost, 3.1.178–79

j

This glide begins with the tongue in the position for the vowel *i:* then
moves into the *j* sound:

you, ye, yon
during, adieu, revenue

When the glide *j* occurs in the middle of a word it is often called
the *liquid u*. The *liquid u* is used in the following words in speaking
Shakespeare:

pew	mute	avenue	value
student	duel	stupid	duke
mutability	debut	new	neutral
renew	nude	adieu	institute
opportunity	ducal	view	dual
volume	Neptune	costume	duet
beautiful	hew	duality	prelude
during	obtuse	endure	futile
tumult	dues	dew	dukedom

No words in English end in this sound.

Alliteration with *j*

- Effects of courtesy, **du**es of grati**tu**de.
- Sir, in**du**ced by my charity
- Oh that she **kne**w she were

Practice Selections for *j*

Will all great Nept**u**ne's ocean wash this blood
Clean from my hand? No, this my hand will rather
The multi**tu**dinous seas incarnadine,
Making the green one red.

Macbeth, 2.2.77–80

OLIVER. Good Mons**ieu**r Charles! What's the **new new**s at the
new court?

CHARLES. There's no **new**s at the court, sir, but the old **new**s;
that is, the old D**u**ke is banished by his younger brother
the **new** D**u**ke; and three or four loving lords have put
themselves in**to** voluntary exile with him, whose lands and
reve**nue**s enrich the **new** D**u**ke; therefore he gives them
good leave to wander.

As You Like It, 1.1.85–91

My noble father,
I **do** perceive here a divided d**u**ty:
To you I am bound for life and ed**u**cation;
My life and ed**u**cation both **do** learn me
How **to** respect **you**; **you** are the lord of d**u**ty;
I am hither**to your** daughter: but here's my husband,
And so much d**u**ty as my mother show'd
To you, preferring **you** before her father,
So much I challenge that I may profess
Due to the Moor my lord.

Othello, 1.3.202–11

The Affricates: tʃ, dʒ

Affricates are two consonants blended together to form one sound.

tʃ

The voiceless affricate *tʃ* is made with the tip of the tongue on the gum ridge for *t*; the breath is then released with the tip of the tongue for the sound *ʃ*, creating *tʃ*, a combination of the two as in *church*.

> chew, choke, chop
> dispatch, Richard, munched
> itch, hatch, search

Alliteration with *tʃ*
- With wit**ch**craft of his wit,
- Beated and **ch**opp'd with tann'd antiquity,
- To see the vaulted ar**ch**, and the ri**ch** crop

dʒ

This sound is voiced and is a combination of *d* and *ʒ* blended together.

> juice, germ, jewel
> adjourned, regiment, besiege
> rage, fadge, allege

Alliteration with *dʒ*
- This rough ma**g**ic I here ab**ju**re.
- **J**ephthah, **j**udge of Israel
- Look on my **George**; I am a **g**entleman.

Use the following pairs of words to practice the difference between the *tʃ* and the *dʒ* sounds.

cheek—jeep   chest—jest   rich—ridge   batches—badges
catches—cages   match—madge   lunch—lunge   search—surge

Don't add the *tʃ-dʒ* sound when a word ending in *t* or *d* is followed by a *y*, as this will make the word sound like *hit chew* or *did jew*. See the following examples of phrases that should *not* use the *tʃ-dʒ* sound.

Fit you   Would you   Let you
Find you   That you   Had you
Meet you   Should you   Sought you
Bid you

Practice Selections for *tʃ*

A sailor's wife had **ch**estnuts in her lap,
And mun**ch**'d, and mun**ch**'d, and mun**ch**'d:—

Macbeth, 1.3.4–5

Urge neither **ch**arity nor shame to me:
Un**ch**aritably with me have you dealt,
And shamefully by you my hopes are but**ch**er'd.
My **ch**arity is outrage, life my shame
And in that shame still live my sorrow's rage.

Richard III, 1.3.281–85

Here feel we not the penalty of Adam,
The seasons' difference; as the icy fang
And **ch**urlish **ch**iding of the winter's wind,

As You Like It, 2.1.5–7

Practice Selections for *dʒ*

Therefore, **J**ew,
Though **j**ustice be thy plea, consider this,
That, in the course of **j**ustice, none of us
Should see salvation . . .

The Merchant of Venice, 4.1.207–10

Let him that thinks of me so ab**j**ectly
Know that this gold must coin a strata**g**em,
Which, cunningly effected, will beget
A very excellent piece of villainy:

Titus Andronicus, 2.3.4–7

Ra**g**e must be withstood:
Give me his ga**g**e: lions make leopards tame.

Richard II, 1.1.178–79

The Syllabic Consonants

A syllabic consonant is a consonant or a group of consonants that forms a syllable. There are no vowels between these consonant combinations, which are pronounced as one sound.

Begin with the nasal consonant *n.* Feel the vibrations on the tip of the tongue and notice the "V" shape under the tongue. This is the muscle that controls the tip of the tongue, and it should be spread slightly for *n* because the tip fans out over the gum ridge, cutting off the sound coming through the mouth and sending it through the nose. Now let the voice intone *l—l—l.* The "V" shape will narrow slightly because the sides of the tongue narrow, allowing the voice to come over the sides of the tongue. Be careful not to tense the back of the tongue, and keep the tip of the tongue firmly on the gum ridge. This is used with other consonants as well when they form an unstresssed syllable of only consonants.

Exercise: **Strengthening the tip of the tongue**

This exercise will help strengthen the tip of the tongue for pronouncing syllabic consonants. Place tip of tongue on the gum ridge and intone *n-l* over and over as in the word *tunnel*:

n—l—n—l—n—l—n—l—n—l
n—l—n—l—n—l—n—l—n—l

Practice Selections for Syllabic Consonants

tl
- my li**ttl**e heart
- Would have made nature immor**tal**
- sub**tle** as the fox for prey,

tn
- swee**ten** this little hand
- Bea**ten**, badly beaten, Hal
- When I was cer**tain** o'er uncertainty

tlz
- Yield stinging ne**ttles** to mine enemies
- Show scarce so gross as bea**tles**
- white-upturnèd wondering eyes of mor**tals**

tnz
- shady cur**tains** from Aurora's bed
- Ere one can say 'It ligh**tens**.'
- Ligh**tens** my humour

dn
- For misery is trod**den** on by many
- else would a mai**den** blush
- par**don** me thou bleeding piece of earth

dl

- these are flowers of mi**ddle** summer
- all the i**dle** weeds that grow
- an old mothy sa**ddle**

dnz

- Is as the mai**den's** organ
- bur**dens** of the prime
- Our bodies are our gar**dens,**

dlz

- who would far**dles** bear
- i**dles** in the wanton summer air
- being ever from their cra**dles**

tld

- a ti**tled** gentleman
- strongly emba**ttled** against me
- Neither enti**tled** in the other's heart.

dld

- and wa**ddled** all about
- ambition that cur**dled** into
- rash and unbri**dled** boy.

tnd

- how have I frigh**tened** thee,
- your mother's cat had but ki**ttened**
- We shall be shor**tened** in our aim,

dln

- take you for i**dleness** itself
- Thrives in our i**dleness**.
- maidens call it love-in-i**dleness**

nl

- in all exter**nal** grace you have some part
- Or hide me nightly in a char**nel** house
- there can be no ker**nel** in this light nut;

ntl

- thy black ma**ntle**
- Lo, here the ge**ntle** lark
- O, he's a lovely ge**ntle**man

ndl

- This is the way to ki**ndle**
- the sca**ndal** vanish with my life
- I know how to ha**ndle** you.

ntld

- E**ntitled** in thy parts do crownèd sit,
- Neither e**ntitled** in the other's heart.
- With an u**ntitled** tyrant bloody-scepter'd,

ndld

- How wert thou ha**ndled** being prisoner?
- kindled duty ki**ndled** her mistrust,
- cause o' the king unha**ndled**;

ndlz

- Night's ca**ndles** are burnt out
- ha**ndles** his bow like a crow-keeper.
- He ki**ndles** a fire

dnl

- Father car**dinal**, I have heard
- Car**dinal**, I'll be no breaker
- Yet let us watch the haughty Car**dinal**;

zn

- corrupts with virtuous sea**son**
- the fresh lap of the crim**son** rose
- in the bla**zon** of sweet beauty's best

znd

- 'Tis an unsea**son'd** courtier
- the encrim**son'd** mood
- fit and sea**soned** for his passage?

sl
- a little pin bores through his ca**stl**e wall
- the thi**stl**e grows underneath the nettle
- Hear the shrill whi**stl**e

zl
- The ou**sel**-cock so black of hue
- As quarrelous as the wea**sel**
- the air doth dri**zzl**e dew;

slz
- strike the ve**ssels**, ho?
- Their coun**sels** and their cares,
- And mor**sels** unctuous,

zlz
- Night-wandering wea**sels**
- pu**zzles** the will,
- it da**zzles** mine eye

sld
- The bri**stled** lips before him:
- Whi**stled** his honour off to the wind

zld
- hath da**zzled** my reason's light;
- dri**zzled** blood upon the capitol
- That have been so beda**zzled**

kl
- when in the chron**icl**e of wasted time
- I would the gods had made thee poet**ical**
- must be caught with t**ickl**ing.

gl
- gaze an ea**gle** blind
- hang my bu**gle**
- you bo**ggle** shrewdly

klz

- Blue cir**cles** stream'd;
- Of these dilated arti**cles** allow.
- His words are bonds, his oaths are ora**cles**,

glz

- The crows to peck the ea**gles**.
- from thence he stru**ggles** to be gone,
- Man**gles** true judgment

kld

- the tender horns of co**ckled** snails
- That monthly changes in her cir**cled** orb
- Encir**cled** you to hear with reverence

gld

- all ha**ggled** over
- Achilles hath invei**gled** his fool
- stru**ggled** in the net

ŋkld

- twi**nkled** on my bastardizing.
- To view with hollow eye and wri**nkled** brow
- Spri**nkled** cool patience!

The English Vowels and Diphthongs

Vowels are open sounds produced by a stream of uninterrupted air vibrating the vocal cords. Diphthongs are two vowels blended together to form one sound.

The Front Vowels: i:, ɪ, e, æ, a

Vowels can be long or short. There is only one long front vowel: the vowel *i:*. In American English, this vowel is made with the lips slightly spread as if for a slight smile, the jaw is high with the tip of the tongue behind the lower front teeth and the front of the tongue arching forward. For the other front vowels, the jaw drops lower and lower from the initial position of *i:* for each vowel.

i:

eat, eel, each
peak, fleece, heap
free, thee, he

- So many **weeks** ere the poor fools will **ean**
- My blessing **season** this in **thee**
- Than I to **speak** my **griefs** unspeakable:

Practice Selections for *i:*

He hath arm'd our answer,
And Florence is denied before he comes:
Yet, for our gentlemen that **mean** to **see**
The Tuscan service, **freely** have they **leave**
To stand on **either** part.

All's Well That Ends Well, 1.2.13–17

I **dream'd** there was an Emperor **Antony**:
O, such another **sleep**, that I might **see**
But such another man!

Antony and Cleopatra, 5.2.104–6

Blind **fear**, that **seeing reason leads**, finds safer footing than blind **reason** stumbling without **fear**: to **fear** the worst oft cures the worse.

Troilus and Cressida, 3.2.74–76

The front vowel *ı* is always short and gives a light rhythmical quality to the character's speech.

> if, ill, is
> fill, sin, rip
> silly, happily, family

Note that just because a word is spelled with the letter *e* doesn't necessarily mean it is pronounced with the sound of the vowel *e*. The following words are all pronounced with the short vowel *ı*:

endure	enough	endow	encumber
entitle	endear	effect	engild

Some examples of phrases pronounced with *ı*:
- Sure, all's **effectless**;
- We will **entice** the Duke of Burgundy
- **Entitled** in thy parts do crownèd sit,

Words that begin with the prefix *ex* in an unstressed syllable are also pronounced with *ı*:

> examine, exclaim, exult
> excuse, explain, experience
> excessive, experiment

Practice the following phrases that include words beginning with *ex*:
- Pawn their **experience** to their present pleasure
- Stay, gentle Helena, hear my **excuse**,
- Say, gentlemen, what makes you thus **exclaim**,

Don't double stress *ı* in words like *enough, effect, eternal, election,* and *effective,* because that will throw off the iambic line.
- When in eternal lines to time thou grow'st.
- From this enormous state,
- Let us go thank him, and encourage him;

Don't lengthen *ı* in prefixes of words:

be: bestow, between, beware, besides, befall
- Tis not so sweet now as it was **before**.
- She did **betray** me to my own reproof
- And my young mistress thus I did **bespeak**:

de: deny, decree, divine, destroy, decline
- **demanded** / My prisoners in your majesty's behalf
- she **derives** her honesty
- well by this **declension**

pre: prevail, pretend, prescribe, preposterous, precipitate
- Lord Angelo is **precise**
- By oft **predict** that I in heaven find
- and dumb **presagers** of my speaking breast

re: remain, reply, receive, return, remembrance
- With my own breath **release** all duteous oaths
- Let me **remember** thee what thou has promised
- thus we die while **remiss** traitors sleep

se: select, serene, severe, seditious, securely
- Our means **secure** us
- Why are you **sequestered** from all your train;
- With eyes **severe** and beard of formal cut

You can use the short *ı* in words with weak syllables in place of the schwa, like *malefaction, epitaph, miraculous,* and *celebrated.*
- With epithets and accents of the Scot
- Our contract celebrated.
- They have proclaim'd their malefactions;

You can also use the short *ı* when pronouncing the *èd* endings of words in lines of verse where an extra syllable is needed to complete the meter.
- Is by a forgèd process of my death
- The eldest son of this distressèd Queen
- Write loyal cantons of contemnèd love

The *less/ness* suffix is always pronounced with an *ɪ*:

goodness	coldness	hardness	boldness
happiness	worldliness	grossness	darkness
faithless	joyless	heartless	hopeless
chapless	hapless	thriftless	senseless

Some examples of phrases with the *less/ness* suffix:
- To be his whore is wit**less**
- You heed**less** joltheads
- Hath made thee hand**less** in thy father's sight?

Practice Selections for *ɪ*

All **is** whole;
Not one word more of the consumèd time.
Let's take the **instant** by the forward top;
For we are old, and on our quick'st **decrees**
The inaudible and **noiseless** foot of Time
Steals **ere** we can **effect** them.

All's Well That Ends Well, 5.3.45–50

You have **prevailed**: I will **depart** in quiet,
And, in **despite** of mirth, mean to be **merry**.

Comedy of Errors, 3.1.130–31

And now **remains**
That we find out the cause of this **effect**—
Or rather say, the cause of this **defect**,
For this **effect defective** comes by cause.
Thus it **remains**, and the **remainder** thus.

Hamlet, 2.2.109–13

The lips are slightly spread for *e*, and it is always short. No words in English end in this sound in spite of the spelling:

> edge, excellent, end
> well, lend, commence

When the prefix *ex* is stressed as in "Therefore exhale," it is pronounced with *e*:

- Thus will I drown your **exclamations**.
- Should presently **extirpate** me and mine
- Now, my co-mates and brothers in **exile**,

Practice Selections for *e*

Friends now fast sworn,
Whose double bosoms seem to wear one heart,
Whose house, whose bed, whose meal, and **exercise**,
Are still together, who twin, as 'twere, in love
Unseparable, shall within this hour,
On a **dissension** of a doit, break out
To **bitterest enmity**:

Coriolanus, 4.4.17–23

Flight cannot stain the honour you have won;
But mine it will, that no **exploit** have done:
You fled for vantage, **everyone** will **swear**;
But, if I bow, they'll say it was for fear.

Henry VI, Part 1, 4.5.25–28

And I in going, madam, weep o'er my father's death
anew: but I must **attend** his majesty's command, to
whom I am now in ward, **evermore** in subjection.

All's Well That Ends Well, 1.1.4–6

The jaw drops and keeps a slight lip spread for *æ*—this sound is always short.

> apple, ask, actor
> battle, chapter, happy

- ravening lamb
- this paragon of animals
- Oh that "had," how sad a passage 'tis!

In American English the *æ* sound is often pronounced with the diphthong ɛɚ as in the word *air*. This can make the assonance difficult to hear in phrases like:

> **Marry**, this well **carried** shall on her behalf
> Change slander to remorse . . .
> *Much Ado about Nothing*, 4.1.218–19

Distinguish between the diphthong ɛɚ (air) and *æ* in the following words:

ɛɚ}—*æ*		
merry—marry	pair—paragon	parent—apparent
care—carriage	Ariel—arrogance	harem—harridan
airy—arrow	care—character	hilarious—Harold
daring—dastardly	fair—fancy	Sarah—sanctity
berry—barricado	share—shaft	bury—barren
fare—fact	tear—tarry	Mary—marrow
hairy—Harry	chary—charity	

Note that *marry* is always pronounced with an *æ* sound whether as an expletive or a verb, which is often pronounced differently in American English.

- Ay, marry, is't.
- Marry, hang you!
- yet, you desire to marry
- I do marry that I may repent.

Notice the wordplay on the word *marry* in the following lines from *Romeo and Juliet*:

> NURSE. Peace, I have done. God mark thee to his grace!
>   Thou wast the prettiest babe that e'er I nursed:
>   An I might live to see thee **married** once,
>   I have my wish.
> LADY CAPULET. **Marry**, that 'marry' is the very theme
>   I came to talk of. Tell me, daughter Juliet,
>   How stands your disposition to be **married**?
>
> *Romeo and Juliet*, 1.3.55–61

Be careful not to nasalize the vowel *æ* before a nasal consonant as in *ham*, *hand*, *hang*:

- The pangs of disprized love
- What did he marry me to famish me
- What a piece of work is a man

Practice Selections for *æ*

> O, bid me leap, rather than **marry** Paris,
> From off the battlements of yonder tower;
>
> *Romeo and Juliet*, 4.1.79–80

> That I, which know my heart, do here pronounce,
> By the very truth of it, I care not for you,
> And am so near the lack of **charity**—
> To accuse myself—I hate you; which I had rather
> You felt than make't my boast.
>
> *Cymbeline*, 2.3.128–32

> And thou **hast** talk'd
> Of **sallies** and retires, of trenches, tents,
> Of palisadoes, frontiers, **parapets**,
> Of basilisks, of **cannon**, culverin,
> Of prisoners' **ransom** and of soldiers slain,
> And all the currents of a heady fight.
>
> *Henry IV, Part 1*, 2.3.51–56

In American Stage Standard Dialect there is something called a "mid-Atlantic" sound regarding the front vowel *a*. In General American English, words like *ask*, *apple*, *bath*, *castle*, and *dance* are pronounced with the *æ* sound. Some American Shakespeare companies prefer to substitute the intermediate, "mid-Atlantic" *a* sound. This practice has been attributed to an attempt to meld the difference between British and American *a* sounds in words like *bath* when a company consists of both North American and British actors, such as the Stratford Festival in Ontario, Canada. The difference between the *æ* and *a* vowel sounds is a matter of dropping the jaw slightly lower, as they are both front vowels. The *a* sound is sometimes referred to as part of the "ask" list: words that are pronounced with *a* in American English and *α:* in British English. Here are some examples (if you are using British English, use the vowel *α:*):

afternoon	after	aft	asked
ask	asketh	ample	aunt
afterwards	answer	plaster	bath
laughter	task	wrath	staff
aghast	last	Falstaff	epitaph
basket	grass	behalf	mask
enchant	chance		

- For you and I are **past** our **dancing** days.
- and weep ye now seeing she is **advanced**
- Free from the **slanders** and this open shame

Practice Selections for *a*

Cheerly to sea; the signs of war **advance**:
No king of England, if not king of **France**.

Henry V, 2.2.195–96

Thou god of this great **vast**, rebuke these surges,
Which wash both heaven and hell; and thou, that **hast**
Upon the winds command, bind them in **brass**,
Having call'd them from the deep!

Pericles, 3.1.1–4

The **hand** could pluck her back that shoved her on.
I must from this **enchanting** queen break off:
Ten thou**sand** harms, more than the ills I know,
My idleness doth **hatch**. How now! Enobarbus!

Antony and Cleopatra, 1.2.141–44

The Middle Vowels: 3:, ə, ʌ

The middle vowels are made with a neutral lip position and with the jaw slightly dropped. The first middle vowel, *3:*, can use *r* coloring, as can the second middle vowel, *ə*, which is always unstressed and usually called the *schwa*. The schwa is always used in *er* word endings: *father, brighter, laughter*. The third middle vowel, *ʌ*, is always used in a stressed syllable.

3:

early, earn, earl
heard, stirred, churl
fur, cur, her

- Than you shall hear the **surly** sullen bell
- the **churlish** chiding of the winter's wind
- Thy company, which **erst** was **irksome** to me,

The first middle vowel *ɜ:* is sometimes pronounced differently today than it was in Shakespeare's time, especially in American English. In contemporary American usage the word *err* is often pronounced *ɛə*, as in the word *air*. In order for a rhymed couplet ending with the *ɜ:* vowel to actually rhyme, it must be pronounced with *ɜ:*.

For example, in this selection from *All's Well That Ends Well,* the rhymed couplet at the end of the King's speech requires "her" and "err" to rhyme.

> As thou lovest **her,**
> Thy love's to me religious; else, does **err.**
> *All's Well That Ends Well,* 2.3.182–83

In *Hamlet,* the Player Queen speaks all her lines in rhymed couplets:

> O, confound the rest!
> Such love must needs be treason in my breast.
> When second husband let me be **accurst!**
> None wed the second but who killed the **first.**
> *Hamlet,* 3.2.184–87

In this text from *A Midsummer Night's Dream*, assonance requires the repeated vowel *ɜ:*.

> He will not know what all but he doth know:
> And as he **errs,** doting on **Hermia's** eyes,
> So I, admiring of this qualities:
> *A Midsummer Night's Dream,* 1.1.240–42

Practice Selection for ɜ:

Thus do they, **sir**: they take the flow o' the Nile
By **certain** scales i' the pyramid; they know,
By the height, the lowness, or the mean, if **dearth**
Or foison follow: the higher Nilus swells,
The more it promises: as it ebbs, the seedsman
Upon the slime and ooze scatters his grain,
And shortly comes to harvest.

Antony and Cleopatra, 2.7.20–26

ə

---

a, an, and, the

Use the schwa for articles, conjunctions, prepositions, and small words on the weak beat that are not given full stress. The schwa is used only in unstressed syllables.

- **A** mot**her** and **a** mistress and **a** friend,
- 'Farewell,' quoth she, '**and** come a**gain to**morrow:
- **And** that which gov**erns** me **to** go a**bout**

Practice Selections for ə

The strawberry grows underneath **the** nettle
And wholesome berries thrive **and** ripen best
Neighbour'd by fruit **of** bas**er** quality:

Henry V, 1.1.99–101

I am robbed, sir, **and** beaten; my money **and** apparel ta'en from me, **and** these detestable things put upon me.

The Winter's Tale, 4.3.64–66

> This is most brave,
> That I, **the** son **of a** dear father murther'd,
> Prompted to my revenge by heaven **and** hell,
> Must (like **a** whore) unpack my heart with words
> **And** fall **a-**cursing like **a** very drab,
> **A** scullion!
>
> *Hamlet*, 2.2.573–78

ʌ

up, ugly, upstart
jug, cup, love

The third middle vowel ʌ is always stressed and used only in stressed syllables and words.

- He was furnished like a **hunter**
- Which, like the toad, **ugly** and venomous
- We'd **jump** the life to **come**.

The vowel ʌ also appears in the old English forms *doth (duth, dʌθ)* and *dost (dust, dʌst)*.

- Tranio, well **dost** thou advise.
- He **doth** bestride the narrow world like a colossus
- The lady **doth** protest too much, methinks.
- coward conscience, how **dost** thou afflict me!

Prefixes with ʌ

un-

- their fitness now does **unmake** you
- I'll **unhair** thy head!
- **unsex** me here

up-

- when he most attains the **upmost** round
- In spite of spite, alone **upholds** the day
- Thou art **uproused** with some distemperature

under-
- thou hast **underwrought** his lawful king
- Who **undertakes** you to your end
- I have by **underhand** means laboured to dissuade him from it

---

Practice Selection for ʌ

Those that Hobgoblin call you and sweet **Puck**,
You do their work, and they shall have good **luck:**
Are not you he?

A Midsummer Night's Dream, 2.1.38–40

The Back Vowels: uː, ʊ, o, ɔː, ɒ, ɑː

The back vowels are shaped with the lips rounded, which lifts the soft palate and brings the jaw forward. This creates a warm, slightly lower pitched series of sounds.

Suck on the end of your finger or a pencil, rounding the lips, then pull it out and say *uː*. Drop the jaw in succession for each of the subsequent back vowel sounds.

---

uː

---

ooze, ouzel
fool, lewd, muse
crew, hue, drew

- How might one **do**, sir, to **lose** it to her own liking?
- **chewing** the **food** of sweet and bitter fancy,
- The **ouzel** cock, so black of **hue**

Practice Selection for *u:*

Give me some **music**; **music**, moody food
Of us that trade in love.

Antony and Cleopatra, 2.5.1–2

ʊ

should, wood, could, hood, withstood, took

- and **would** within this **wood**
- With that she sighed as she **stood**,
- many likeli**hoods** informed me of this

Practice Selection for ʊ

One **good** woman in ten, madam; which is a purifying
o' the song: **would** God **would** serve the world so all
the year! we'ld find no fault with the tithe-woman,
if I were the parson. One in ten, quoth a'!

All's Well That Ends Well, 1.3.87–89

o

opine, Ophelia, opprest, Olivia, Orodes

The *o* sound is used only in an unstressed syllable. It is the first
sound in the diphthong *oʊ̆*, which is used in stressed syllables such as
"oh," "groan," and "foe." In contemporary American usage, the short
o is usually replaced with the schwa (*ə*).

- I saw **O**thello's visage in his mind
- lust, as **O**bidicut
- And call him 'madam,' do him **o**beisance

ɔː

all, autumn, Albany, sauce, cause
lawyer, paw, flaw, draw

- How **called** you the man you speak of, madam?
- How **long** is't ago, Jack, since thou **sawest** thine own knee?
- That doth with **awe** and terror kneel to it!

Practice Selection for ɔː

I am **all** the **daughters** of my father's house,
And **all** the brothers too: and yet I know not.

Twelfth Night, 2.4.130–31

ɒ

honor, oracle, orange, orison
hob, conquer, stop

Keep this sound slightly rounded and don't substitute the last back
vowel *αː*.

- I'll **stop** mine ears against the mermaids **song**.
- As by **lot**, **God wot** and then you know.
- We shall **not** find like **opportunity**.

Practice Selection for ɒ

O **Cromwell, Cromwell**!
Had I but served my **God** with half the zeal
I served my king, he would **not** in mine age
Have left me naked to mine enemies.

Henry VIII, 3.2.541–44

alms, almond, arm
calm, palm, psalm,
pa, ha

- When such strings **jar** what hope of **harmony**?
- **Calmly** I do beseech you.
- Death, as **Psalmist** saith, is certain to all;

Practice Selection for *ɑː*:

Ah, let be, let be! thou **art**
The **armourer** of my **heart**:

Antony and Cleopatra, 4.4.9–10

Nought (ɔː) versus Not (ɒ)

Be sure to distinguish between the two back vowels ɔː and ɒ in the words *nought* and *not*. They are slightly different, and Shakespeare makes wordplay with the difference.

I have stol'n **nought**, nor would **not**, though I had found
Gold strew'd i' the floor.

Cymbeline, 3.6.56–57

Yet can I **not** of such tame patience boast
As to be hush'd and **nought** at all to say:

Richard II, 1.1.55–56

Yet hold I off. Women are angels, wooing:
Things won are done; joy's soul lies in the doing.
That she beloved knows **nought** that knows **not** this:

Troilus and Cressida, 1.2.285–87

The Diphthongs: eĭ, aĭ, ɔĭ, oŏ, aŏ

Diphthongs are combinations of two vowels sounded together. The first element is stressed while the second is weaker, as shown by the symbol ˘. The first two diphthongs, *eĭ* and *aĭ*, are slightly spread front vowels; the third, *ɔĭ*, consists of a rounded back vowel and a spread front vowel; and the final two, *oŏ* and *aŏ*, are made up of two back vowels.

eĭ—bay
aĭ—buy
ɔĭ—boy
oŏ—bow
aŏ—bough

eĭ

aid, ague, age
bane, slake, trade
lay, may, say

- **take aim against** a sea of troubles
- **Age** cannot wither her, nor custom **stale**
- I pray you, **stay** not, but in **haste** to horse.

aĭ

I, isle, ides
fine, dial, shine
sigh, die, lie

- Enough to purchase such another **island**,
- Doth the moon **shine** that **night** we play our play?
- Than is the coal of **fire** upon the **ice**,

ɔ̆

oil, oyster, oily
toil, boiled, soil
annoy, toy, cloy

- The **garboils** she awaked;
- **Destroy** what lies before 'em.
- be loath to **foil** him, as I must, for my own honour,

ŏ

oh, oak, oat
boat, loathe, toad
woe, so, low

- For do but stand upon the **foaming** shore,
- and you **crow**, cock, with your **comb** on.
- wherein the spirit held his **wont** to walk

ă

owl, out, ounce
bout, loud, howl
now, bow, sow

- Stay but a little, for my **cloud** of dignity
- But **out**, alack, he as but one **hour** mine;
- Now I do **frown** on thee with all my heart;

The Diphthongs of r: ɪɚ̆, ɛɚ̆, ʊɚ̆, ɔɚ̆, ɑɚ̆

There are five diphthongs of *r* in American English that are used only in words ending in the letter *r*.

> ɪɚ̆—fear
> ɛɚ̆—fair
> ʊɚ̆—fewer
> ɔɚ̆—four
> ɑɚ̆—far

If the word ends with a consonant following the *r* (as in *hard*), or the next word or syllable begins with a consonant, the *r* is not pronounced as strongly as in the initial *r* in a word:

> far from
> are you
> star struck
> hard core

If the following word or the next syllable begins with a vowel, the *r* is elided:

> far away
> terrorism
> care of
> pour it

In British English or Received Pronunciation, the *r* is dropped at the end of a word or before a consonant:

> far
> hard
> court
> peer

ear, earring, earshot
weird, feared, cheerily
seer, dear, here

- Grief would have **tears**, and sorrow bids me speak
- That high All-**Seer** that I dallied with
- Is she, my liege, can make me know this **clearly**,

ɛə̆

air, e'er, heir
paired, sharing, tearing
lair, dare, ne'er

- It is like a barber's **chair** that fits all buttocks,
- In that and all your worthiest **affairs**.
- Now he'll **outstare** the lightning.

ʊə̆

ewer
cured, touring, lurid
poor, fewer, tour

- Led hither by **pure** love:
- Not so **allured** to feed.
- It is much that the **Moor** should be more than reason:

ɔə̆

oar, o'er, or
scored, pours, coarsely
boar, roar, core

- Reports but **coarsely** of her.
- **Aboard** my galley I invite you all:
- He cried almost to **roaring**.

ǎɔ̌

are, arc, argal
bark, target, depart
star, scar, far

- Ay, with all my **heart**; and thou **art** worthy of it.
- and this morning your **departure** hence,
- Lady, of that I have made a bold **charter**;

Practice Selections for Diphthongs of *r*

Come, thou **monarch** of the vine,
Plumpy Bacchus with pink eyne!
In thy fats **our cares** be drown'd,
With thy **grapes our hairs** be crown'd:
Cup us, till the **world** go **round**,
Cup us, till the **world** go **round**!

Antony and Cleopatra, 2.7.142–47

All that **glitters** is not gold;
Often have you **heard** that told:
Many a man his life hath sold
But my outside to behold:
Gilded tombs do **worms** enfold.
Had you been as wise as bold,
Young in limbs, in judgment old,
Your answer had not been **inscroll'd**:
Fare you well; **your** suit is cold.

Merchant of Venice, 2.7.67–75

> **Certain**, 'tis **certain**; **very sure**, **very sure**. Death, as Psalmist
> saith, is **certain** to all; all shall die. How a good of bullocks at
> **Stamford** fair?
>
> *Henry IV, Part 2*, 3.2.47–49

Weak Forms in Shakespeare

In English, *weak forms* are an unstressed variation on a strong form
of a word. Articles, prepositions, conjunctions, and auxiliary verbs
are in this category. When speaking Shakespeare's text, an actor
should not stress these words if they fall on the weak beat. This
doesn't mean that these words are never stressed; it just means that
stressing them is unusual and calls attention to the word, as in "you
may have **a** cake"—meaning one cake. Here are some examples of
weak forms:

> **The** strawberry grows underneath **the** nettle, [articles]
> **And** wholesome berries thrive **and** ripen best [conjunctions]
> Neighbour'd **by** fruit **of** baser quality: [prepositions]
>
> *Henry V*, 1.1.99–101

Connectives: and

Some American actors tend to stress *and* on the weak beat, which
throws off the rhythm of the verse and makes the simple article *and*
the focus. In the example below, placing a stress on *and* would take
the emphasis off *stole*, which is where the stress belongs.

> Towards him I made, but he was ware of me
> And stóle intó the cóvert óf the wóod:
>
> *Romeo and Juliet*, 1.1.145–46

When you have a line with a number of phrases connected by *and*, be careful that you don't overemphasize *and*. Make the schwa sound *ə* (*'un* or *'n*) rather than the strong, or stressed, form of the word.

- Up **and** down, up **and** down,
- **And** thanks, **And** ever thanks
- Sith I have cause, **and** will, **and** strength, **and** means to do't

Other Sample Connectives

from
- And every fair **from** fair sometime declines.
- A native slip to us **from** foreign seeds:
- I am **from** humble, he **from** honour'd name;

of
- What hope is there **of** his majesty's amendment?
- What is it, my good lord, the king languishes **of**?
- The Jove **of** power make me most weak,

could
- Ay me! For aught that I **could** ever read,
- You saw one here in court **could** witness it.
- And willingly **could** waste my time in it.

for
- That's **for** advantage.
- **For** what good turn?
- And all in war with time **for** love of you,

an, a
- I am **a** man whom fortune hath cruelly scratched.
- Is not this **a** strange fellow
- **an** unclean mind carries virtuous qualities,

the
- He cannot want **the** best
- **The** ambition in my love thus plagues itself:
- 'tis against **the** rule of nature.

on

- I think not **on** my father;
- Cold wisdom waiting **on** superfluous folly.
- To stand **on** either part.

Practice Selections for Connectives

> Ah, what sharp stings are in her mildest words!
> Rinaldo, you did never lack advice so much,
> As letting her pass so: had I spoke with her,
> I **could** have well diverted her intents,
> Which thus she hath prevented.
>
> *All's Well That Ends Well*, 3.4.18–22

> 'Tis the best brine **a** maiden can season her praise in. **The** remembrance **of** her father never approaches her heart but **the** tyranny **of** her sorrows takes all livelihood **from** her cheek.
>
> *All's Well That Ends Well*, 1.1.45–49

> Tut, I can counterfeit **the** deep tragedian;
> Speak and look back, **and** pry **on** every side,
> Tremble **and** start at wagging **of a** straw,
> Intending deep suspicion: ghastly looks
> Are at my service, like enforced smiles;
> **And** both are ready in their offices,
> At any time, to grace my stratagems.
> But what, is Catesby gone?
>
> *Richard III*, 3.5.5–12

4

Shakespeare's Language: Rhetoric

Elizabethan Rhetoric

The Elizabethans were educated in a wide variety of the forms of rhetoric, or the use of language to persuade through public speaking. Rhetoric was taught in all the grammar schools, and Shakespeare's education would have encompassed a thorough grounding in all its myriad forms. According to Wilbur Samuel Howell,

> Rhetoric was regarded in England at that time as the theory behind the statements intended for the populace. Since the populace consisted of laymen and since the speaker was to some extent a master of the real technicalities of his subject, rhetoric was regarded as the theory of communication between the learned and the lay world or between expert and layman.[1]

Follow the Argument

Most of Shakespeare's speeches present an opening argument, which is then explored and expanded, using all the intellectual and emotional resources of the speaker to resolve or conclude the argument.

In *Richard II*, for example, King Richard has been imprisoned by his cousin Henry Bolingbrook, who wants to depose Richard and set himself on the throne. From his prison cell, the king contemplates and tries to make sense of his situation.

> I have been studying how I may compare
> This prison where I live unto the world:
> And for because the world is populous
> And here is not a creature but myself,
> I cannot do it; yet I'll hammer it out.
> My brain I'll prove the female to my soul,
> My soul the father; and these two beget
> A generation of still-breeding thoughts,
> And these same thoughts people this little world,
> In humours like the people of this world,
> For no thought is contented. The better sort,
> As thoughts of things divine, are intermix'd
> With scruples and do set the word itself
> Against the word:
> As thus, 'Come, little ones,' and then again,
> 'It is as hard to come as for a camel
> To thread the postern of a small needle's eye.'
>
> *Richard II*, 5.5.1–16

Rhetoric Spoken by Shakespeare's Contemporaries

In the Elizabethan world, the general public, of whom a large majority were illiterate, were used to listening to all forms of rhetoric in their daily lives. Attendance at church was mandatory, with sermons often lasting two to three hours. Speeches in Parliament were supported by arguments using a wide variety of rhetorical devices, as were the speeches of the nobility and royalty.

Elizabeth I

Elizabeth I, probably one of the most brilliant and highly educated monarchs ever to occupy the throne of England, famously said in a speech to Parliament, "I thank God I am indeed endowed with such qualities that if I were turned out of the realm in my petticoat I were able to live in any place in Christendom."[2]

The following is a transcript of the speech she gave on horseback to her troops at Tilbury during that attempted invasion of England by the Spanish Armada:

> My loving people,
>
> I have been persuaded by some that are careful of my safety to take heed how I committed myself to armed multitudes, for fear of treachery. But I tell you that I would not desire to live to distrust my faithful and loving people. Let tyrants fear: I have so behaved myself that under God I have placed my chiefest strength and safeguard in the loyal hearts and goodwill of my subjects. Wherefore I am come among you at this time but for my recreation and pleasure, being resolved in the midst and heat of the battle to live and die amongst you all, to lay down for my God and for my kingdom and for my people mine honor and my blood even in the dust. I know I have the body but of a weak and feeble woman, but I have the heart and stomach of a king and of a king of England too—and take foul scorn that Parma or any prince of Europe should dare to invade the borders of my realm. To the which rather than any dishonor shall grow by me, I myself will venter my royal blood; I myself will be your general, judge, and rewarder of your virtue in the field. I know that already for your forwardness you have deserved rewards and crowns, and I assure you in the word of a prince you shall not fail of them. In the meantime, my lieutenant general shall be in my stead, than whom never prince commanded a more noble or worthy subject. Not doubting but by your concord in the camp and valor in the field and your obedience to myself and my general, we shall shortly have a famous victory over these enemies of my God and of my kingdom.[3]

The British actress Glenda Jackson gives an inspired delivery of this speech in the 1971 BBC series *Elizabeth R*.[4]

Sir Walter Raleigh

Even at an execution, the condemned was expected to make a speech, following a prescribed form and with the words recorded for posterity.

Sir Walter Raleigh was a favorite courtier of Elizabeth I, who gave him permission to found the first English colony in the New World. According to historians, he named Virginia after Elizabeth, who was known as "The Virgin Queen."[5] Soldier, sailor, statesman, historian, and explorer, Raleigh could be said to represent the ultimate English Renaissance man. He was also considered a pirate by the Spanish, because he captured Spanish treasure ships and shared the booty with the queen. After Elizabeth's death, James I, her successor, was trying to make peace with Spain and took a rather different view of Raleigh's piracy. After Raleigh attacked a Spanish colonial outpost in what is now Venezuela, James had him executed. On the scaffold, Raleigh made a rather long speech, defending himself on a series of charges that had been laid against him, including conniving in the death of the Earl of Essex. Before he lay his head on the block, he asked to see the ax, and running his finger across the blade, he remarked, "'Tis a sharp medicine, but a sound cure for all diseases." On being told that his head on the block should face east, he said, "It mattered little how the head lay provided the heart was right."[6]

Raleigh, like many Elizabethan aristocrats, was also a poet. This poem was written by Raleigh the night before his execution:

> E'en such is time! who takes in trust
> Our youth, our joys, and all we have,
> And pays us but with age and dust:
> Who, in the dark and silent grave,
> When we have wander'd all our ways,
> Shuts up the story of our days!
> But from this earth, this grave, this dust,
> The Lord will raise me up, I trust.[7]

Anne Boleyn

The following are the final words on the scaffold of Anne Boleyn, the mother of Elizabeth I:

> Good Christian people, I am come hither to die, according to law, for by the law I am judged to die, and therefore I will speak nothing against it. I come here only to die, and thus to yield myself humbly to the will of the King, my lord. And if, in my life, I did ever offend the King's Grace, surely with my

death I do now atone. I come hither to accuse no man, nor to speak anything of that whereof I am accused, as I know full well that aught I say in my defence doth not appertain to you. I pray and beseech you all, good friends, to pray for the life of the King, my sovereign lord and yours, who is one of the best princes on the face of the earth, who has always treated me so well that better could not be, wherefore I submit to death with good will, humbly asking pardon of all the world. If any person will meddle with my cause, I require them to judge the best. Thus I take my leave of the world, and of you, and I heartily desire you all to pray for me. Oh Lord, have mercy on me! To God I commend my soul.[8]

Anne also is said to have written the following poem while imprisoned in the Tower of London and awaiting her execution:

> Oh, death! rock me on sleep,
> Bring me on quiet rest;
> Let pass my very guiltless ghost
> Out of my careful breast.
> Toll on the passing bell,
> Ring out the doleful knell,
> Let the sound of my death tell;
> For I must die,
> There is no remedy,
> For now I die.[9]

Notice how the speech of Hermione, the condemned queen in *The Winter's Tale*, bears some similarities in that she uses rhetoric to work in her defense:

> Sir, spare your threats:
> The bug which you would fright me with I seek.
> To me can life be no commodity:
> The crown and comfort of my life, your favour,
> I do give lost; for I do feel it gone,
> But know not how it went. My second joy
> And first-fruits of my body, from his presence
> I am barr'd, like one infectious. My third comfort

Starr'd most unluckily, is from my breast,
The innocent milk in its most innocent mouth,
Haled out to murder: myself on every post
Proclaimed a strumpet: with immodest hatred
The child-bed privilege denied, which 'longs
To women of all fashion; lastly, hurried
Here to this place, i' the open air, before
I have got strength of limit. Now, my liege,
Tell me what blessings I have here alive,
That I should fear to die? Therefore proceed.
But yet hear this: mistake me not; no life,
I prize it not a straw, but for mine honour,
Which I would free, if I shall be condemn'd
Upon surmises, all proofs sleeping else
But what your jealousies awake, I tell you
'Tis rigor and not law. Your honours all,
I do refer me to the oracle:
Apollo be my judge!

The Winter's Tale, 3.2.97–122

Rhetoric in Elizabethan Education

Playwright Ben Jonson, both a rival and a friend of Shakespeare's, wrote a memorial poem praising him in the edition of the First Folio, in which he said:

> To draw no envy, Shakespeare, on thy name,
> Am I thus ample to thy book and fame;
> . . . .
> And though thou hadst small Latin and less Greek,
> From thence to honour thee I would not seek
> For names; but call forth thundering Aeschylus,
> Euripides, and Sophocles to us,[10]

This allusion to Shakespeare's "small Latin and less Greek" is often used by some critics to prove that Shakespeare was uneducated, although being compared to Aeschylus, Euripides, and Sophocles rather than to contemporary poets like Kyd and Marlowe is no small thing. Jonson was a university man who was classically educated at

118

Cambridge University, where classes at the time were given exclusively in Latin.[11]

However, according to Sister Miriam Joseph in her book *Shakespeare's Use of the Arts of Language*, Jonson meant that Shakespeare had the typical grammar school education of his time, which would seem inconceivably daunting to most schoolchildren today.

Here, Sister Miriam describes the typical grammar school day:

> The order of the day in the Tudor grammar schools prescribed rising at five; class from six to nine; breakfast; class from nine-fifteen to eleven; dinner; class from one to five; supper. After supper, from six to seven, the pupils recited to their fellows what they had learned during the day. The lessons drilled on in the morning were regularly recited in the afternoon, and all the work of the week was reviewed in recitation on Fridays and Saturdays. A week devoted to repetitions tested the accomplishments of the thirty-six weeks of the school year. A sixteenth century schoolmaster estimated that one hour of instruction would require at least six hours of exercise to apply the principles to writing and speaking.[12]

According to Sister Miriam, the aim of the "program of studies" pursued by Elizabethan schoolboys during such an arduous day was,

> to enable the student to read, write, and speak Latin, to acquaint him with the leading Latin classics and a few of the Greek, and to infuse into him sound moral and religious principles. The method prescribed unremitting exercise in grammar, rhetoric, and logic. Grammar dominated the lower forms, logic and rhetoric the upper. In all forms the order was first to learn precepts, then to employ them as a tool of analysis in reading, and finally to use them as a guide in composition.[13]

Through such a method, Elizabethan students learned the more than two hundred figures of speech set forth in Latin handbooks of rhetoric written by Susenbrotus, Erasmus, and Quintilian, figures described in English handbooks by such writers as Thomas Wilson, Abraham Fraunce, Henry Peacham, and George Puttenham. Sister Miriam demonstrates convincingly that knowledge of the rhetorical figures (along with knowledge of the precepts of logic and grammar and of an array of classical writers) laid the foundation for much of Shakespeare's poetic art.

Principal Elizabethan Rhetorical Figures

Following are some of the principal figures of rhetoric that would have been taught in Elizabethan grammar schools.[14]

Anaphora

Reinforcing the meaning in a line of text by repeating the same word at the beginning of each clause or sentence.

> **This** royal throne of kings, this scepter'd isle,
> **This** earth of majesty, this seat of Mars,
> **This** other Eden, demi-paradise,
>
> *Richard II*, 2.1. 40–42

Anastrophe

Inversion of the expected word order.

> Her mother is the lady of the house,
> And a good lady, and a wise and virtuous.
> I nursed her daughter, that you talk'd withal;
> I tell you, he that can lay hold of her
> Shall have the chinks.
>
> *Romeo and Juliet*, 1.5.114–18

Antanaclasis

Using the same word for a different meaning; a pun.

> To England will I **steal**, and there I'll **steal**:
> And patches will I get unto these cudgell'd scars,
> And swear I got them in the Gallia wars.
>
> *Henry V*, 5.1.90–92

Antithesis

Words that are paired as opposites.

> As for you,
> Say what you can, my **false** o'erweighs your **true**.
>
> *Measure for Measure*, 2.4.183–84

Anthypophora

Asking oneself questions and answering them.

> What is honour? A word. What is in that word honour? what
> is that 'honour? air. A trim reckoning! Who hath it? he that
> died o' Wednesday. Doth he feel it? no. Doth he hear it? no.
> 'Tis insensible, then? Yea, to the dead. But will it not live with
> the living? no. Why? detraction will not suffer it. Therefore,
> I'll none of it. Honour is a mere scutcheon: and so ends my
> catechism.
>
> *Henry IV, Part 1*, 5.1.134–40

Aporia

Deliberating and questioning oneself.

> What's in a name? that which we call a rose
> By any other name would smell as sweet;
>
> *Romeo and Juliet*, 2.2.43–44

Brachylogia

Reducing extraneous meaning by omitting conjunctions.

> ATTENDANT. News, my good lord, from Rome.
> ANTONY. Grates me: the sum.
>
> *Antony and Cleopatra*, 1.1.18–19

Catachresis

The use of mixed metaphors for rhetorical effect.

> His complexion is perfect gallows.
>
> *The Tempest*, 1.1.35–36

Chronographia

The metaphorical description of time.

> Night's candles are burnt out, and jocund day
> Stands tiptoe on the misty mountain tops.
>
> *Romeo and Juliet*, 3.5.9–10

Dirimens Copulatio

An initial sentence with an exception in it, followed by another sentence that makes a stronger point than the first.

> Harry, I do not only marvel where thou spendest thy time, but also how thou art accompanied:
>> *Henry IV, Part 1*, 2.4.396–97

Enallage

Deliberate use of one case, person, gender, number, tense, or mood for another.

> What! a young knave, and begging! Is there not wars? Is there not employment? Doth not the King lack subjects?
>> *Henry IV, Part 2*, 1.2.93–94

Encomion

High praise for someone or something.

> Fair Portia's counterfeit! What demi-god
> Hath come so near creation?
>> *Merchant of Venice*, 3.2.115–16

Enumeration

A rhetorical device for listing things in order.

> Marry, sir, they have committed false report; moreover, they have spoken untruths; secondarily, they are slanders; sixth and lastly, they have belied a lady; thirdly, they have verified unjust things; and, to conclude, they are lying knaves.
>> *Much Ado about Nothing*, 5.1.223–28

Epizeuxis

Words or phrases are repeated in quick succession, usually with no words in between.

> O horror, horror, horror! Tongue nor heart
> Cannot conceive nor name thee!
>
> *Macbeth*, 2.3.66–67

Hypallage

The word order is confused and sometimes made absurd.

> Find them out whose names are written here! It is written, that the shoemaker should meddle with his yard, and the tailor with his last, the fisher with his pencil, and the painter with his nets; but I am sent to find those persons whose names are here writ, and can never find what names the writing person hath here writ.
>
> *Romeo and Juliet*, 1.2.38–44

Hysteron Proteron

The natural order of words is reversed.

> The Antoniad, the Egyptian admiral,
> With all their sixty, fly and turn the rudder:
>
> *Antony and Cleopatra*, 3.10.13–14

Isocolon

In rhetoric, the use of phrases or sentences of equal length.

> My lord, we have
> Stood here observing him: some strange commotion
> Is in his brain: he bites his lip, and starts;

Stops on a sudden, looks upon the ground,
Then lays his finger on his temple, straight
Springs out into fast gait; then stops again,
Strikes his breast hard, and anon he casts
His eye against the moon: in most strange postures
We have seen him set himself.

King Henry VIII, 3.2.113–20

Metonymy

The substitution of subject for object or object for subject.

But know, thou noble youth,
The serpent that did sting thy father's life
Now wears his crown.

Hamlet, 1.5.38–40

Optatio

A passionate request, prayer, or wish.

Why, look you, how you storm!
I would be friends with you, and have your love,

Merchant of Venice, 1.3.137–38

Parenthesis

An initial phrase or sentence that could stand alone, interrupted with
a second phrase set off by commas or parentheses.

For brave Macbeth—well he deserves that name—
Distaining fortune, with his brandish'd steel,

Macbeth, 1.2.16–17

Prosopopoeia

The attribution of human qualities to dumb or inanimate creatures or objects.

> The iron tongue of midnight hath told twelve:
> Lovers, to bed; 'tis almost fairy time.
>> *A Midsummer Night's Dream*, 5.1.372–73

Synecdoche

When a part stands for the whole of something or vice versa.

> Take thy face hence.
>> *Macbeth*, 5.3.19

Threnos

A lyrical lament over the victim of a tragedy.

> O, wither'd is the garland of the war,
> The soldier's pole is fall'n: young boys and girls
> Are level now with men; the odds is gone,
> And there is nothing left remarkable
> Beneath the visiting moon.
>> *Antony and Cleopatra*, 4.15.64–68

Topographia

The description of places.

> This castle hath a pleasant seat; the air
> Nimbly and sweetly recommends itself
> Unto our gentle senses.
>> *Macbeth*, 1.6.1–3

Zeugma

One verb or preposition that joins two other words or clauses, usually with different meanings.

> Golden lads and girls all must,
> As chimney-sweepers, come to dust.

Cymbeline, 4.2.262–63

Rhetoric for Contemporary Shakespearean Actors

Fortunately, performing Shakespeare's text doesn't require a deep knowledge of classical rhetoric. However, it can be helpful when approaching a part to see how the rhetoric works in a difficult speech and to use it as one way to discover and gain insight into your character. The following are the principal rhetorical devices used by contemporary Shakespearean actors.

Alliteration

Alliteration is the repetition of the same initial consonant in several words of a sentence. It was one of the primary literary devices in Anglo-Saxon poetry, and featured in the great English epic *Beowulf*:

> **B**loody the **b**illows were **b**oiling there,
> **t**urbid the **t**ide of **t**umbling waves
> **h**orribly seething with sword-blood **h**ot.

Beowulf[15]

The emphasis on the consonants drives the rhythm. Shakespeare does a similar thing in the Pyramus and Thisby scene from *A Midsummer Night's Dream*.

> Whereat, with **b**lade, with **b**loody **b**lameful **b**lade,
> He **b**ravely **b**roach'd his **b**oiling **b**loody **b**reast;

A Midsummer Night's Dream, 5.1.159–60

Alliteration in Verse

> And the **d**eep-**d**rawing barks **d**o there **d**isgorge
> Their warlike fraughtage: now on **D**ardan plains
> The fresh and yet unbruise**d** Greeks do **p**itch
> Their brave **p**avilions . . .
>
> *Troilus and Cressida*, prologue.12–15

> A sailor's wife had **ch**estnuts in her lap,
> And mun**ch**'d, and mun**ch**'d, and mun**ch**'d:—
>
> *Macbeth*, 1.3.4–5

> These are but **w**ild and **w**hirling **w**ords, my lord.
>
> *Hamlet*, 1.5.146

Alliteration in Prose

Shakespeare even uses alliteration in prose, as in the following examples:

> **Sp**eak the **sp**eech, I **p**ray you, as I **p**ronounc'd it to you, trip-**p**ingly on the tongue.
>
> *Hamlet*, 3.2.1–2

> A man that had a **w**ife **w**ith such a **w**it, he might say, '**W**it, **wh**ither **w**ilt?'
>
> *As You Like It*, 4.1.138–39

> BENEDICK. What, my dear Lady **D**isdain! are you yet living?
> BEATRICE. Is it possible **d**isdain should **d**ie while she hath such
>   meet food to feed it as Signior Bene**d**ick? **C**ourtesy itself
>   must **c**onvert to **d**isdain, if you come in her presence.
>
> *Much Ado about Nothing*, 1.1.106–10

Antithesis

Antithesis is quite simply the use of words or phrases that are contrasting. It is a figure of speech that we use every day for emphasis. Notice that the contrasting words are matched in pitch, and that to stress one word at the expense of the other changes the meaning, for example, *back* and forth.

> hot and cold
> black and white
> up and down
> right and left

Antithesis in Verse

- I had rather give my **body** than my **soul**.
- **heaven** and **earth** must I remember
- my **false** o'erweighs your **true**

> John, to stop Arthur's title in the **whole**,
> Hath willingly departed with a **part**,
>
> *King John*, 2.1.586–87

> How far that little candle throws his beams!
> So shines a **good** deed in a **naughty** world.
>
> *The Merchant of Venice*, 5.1.102–3

> Alas, poor Proteus! thou hast entertain'd
> A **fox** to be the shepherd of thy **lambs**.
>
> *Two Gentlemen of Verona*, 4.4.96–97

Antithesis can involve more than one set of contrasting words:

> I cannot tell: the world is grown so bad,
> That **wrens** make **prey** where **eagles** dare not **perch**:
>
> *Richard III*, 1.3.71–72

> From a **resolved** and **honourable war**,
> To a most **base** and **vile-concluded peace**.
>
> *King John*, 2.1.609–10

My only **love** sprung from my only **hate**!
Too **early** seen **unknown**, and **known** too **late**!

Romeo and Juliet, 1.5.149–50

Note that Shakespeare uses antithesis to clarify the sense of the speech: *but* is always antithesis; *yet* is probably antithesis.

Yet weep that Harry's **dead**, and so will I;
But Harry **lives** that shall convert those **tears**
By number into hours of **happiness**.

Henry IV, Part 2, 5.2.62–64

Antithesis in Prose

You will find that Shakespeare uses antithesis in prose just as he does in verse. Treat the pair of words as you would antithesis in verse—pick each of them up and match the pitch.

After your **death** you were better have a bad **epitaph** than their **ill report** while you **live**.

Hamlet, 2.2.514–15

Now this overdone, or come tardy off, though it make the **unskilful laugh**, cannot but make the **judicious grieve**;

Hamlet, 3.2.20–22

Besides this **nothing** that he so plentifully **gives** me, the **something** that nature gave me his countenance seems to **take** from me.

As You Like It, 1.1.14–16

Antithesis in Dialogue

HAMLET. Horatio!—or I do forget myself.

HORATIO. The same, my lord, and your poor **servant** ever.

HAMLET. Sir, my good **friend**—I'll change that name with you.
And what make you from Wittenberg, Horatio?

. . . .

HORATIO. My lord, I came to see your **father's funeral**.

HAMLET. I prithee do not mock me, fellow student.
I think it was to see my **mother's wedding**.

Hamlet, 1.2.166–69, 181–83

ANGELO. Then must your brother die.

ISABELLA. And 'twere the cheaper way:
Better it were a **brother** died at **once**,
Than that a **sister**, by redeeming him,
Should die **for ever**.

ANGELO. Were not you then as cruel as the sentence
That you have slander'd so?

ISABELLA. **Ignomy** in **ransom** and **free pardon**
Are of two houses: **lawful mercy**
Is nothing kin to **foul redemption**.

Measure for Measure, 2.4.114–23

SIR OLIVER. Is there none here to **give** the woman?

TOUCHSTONE. I will not **take** her on gift of any man.

As You Like It, 3.3.53–54

Antithesis in Metaphor

Now is the **winter** of our discontent
Made glorious **summer** by this son of York;

Richard III, 1.1.1–2

Parenthetical Phrases

Some of Shakespeare's speeches have a parenthetical phrase, where the character starts speaking and then changes the direction of his speech before picking up the initial thought again. He may be speaking to himself or to another person. It is set off by commas, dashes, or parentheses. Take a quick breath before and after it, keeping the thought moving with an upward inflection until going on with the initial thought.

Parenthetical Phrases in Verse

> For brave Macbeth—well he deserves that name—
> Disdaining fortune, with his brandish'd steel,
>
> *Macbeth*, 1.2.17–18

> Rebellious subjects, enemies to peace,
> Profaners of this neighbour-stained steel,—
> Will they not hear? What, ho! you men, you beasts,
>
> *Romeo and Juliet*, 1.1.101–3

> This land of such dear souls, this dear dear land,
> Dear for her reputation through the world,
> Is now leased out, I die pronouncing it,
> Like to a tenement or pelting farm:
>
> *Richard II*, 2.1.57–60

Parenthetical Phrases in Dialogue

> FRIAR LAURENCE. Arise; one knocks; good Romeo, hide thyself.
> ROMEO. Not I; unless the breath of heartsick groans,
>   Mist-like, infold me from the search of eyes.
> FRIAR LAURENCE. Hark, how they knock! Who's there?
>   Romeo, arise;
>   Thou wilt be taken. Stay awhile! Stand up;
>   Run to my study. By and by! God's will,
>   What simpleness is this! I come, I come!
>
> *Romeo and Juliet*, 3.3.75–81

woe upon ye
And all such false professors! would you have me—
If you have any justice, any pity;
If ye be any thing but churchmen's habits—
Put my sick cause into his hands that hates me?

Henry VIII, 3.1.131–35

Parenthetical Phrases in Prose

I will deliver his challenge by word of mouth; set upon Aguecheek a notable report of valour; and drive the gentleman, as I know his youth will aptly receive it, into a most hideous opinion of his rage, skill, fury and impetuosity.

Twelfth Night, 3.4.186–90

I do affect the very ground, which is base, where her shoe, which is baser, guided by her foot, which is basest, doth tread.

Love's Labour's Lost, 1.2.153–55

Repetition

Mad world! **mad** kings! **mad** composition!

King John, 2.1.585

Not a whit, we defy augury; there's a special providence in the fall of a sparrow. **If it be now**, 'tis **not to come**; **if it be not to come**, **it will be now**; **if it be not now**, yet **it will come**: the readiness is all. Since no man knows aught of what he leaves, what is't to leave betimes?

Hamlet, 5.2.203–7

O virtuous fight,
When **right** with **right** wars who shall be most **right**!

Troilus and Cressida, 3.2.173–74

Rhetorical Questions

A rhetorical question is a question asked for effect; it isn't intended as a question requiring an answer. However, you must ask the question and not just make a statement.

- What early tongue so sweet saluteth me?
- Did ever dragon keep so fair a cave?
- Is this your Christian counsel?

Rhetorical Questions in Verse

> Is this a dagger which I see before me,
> **The handle toward my hand?**
>
> *Macbeth*, 2.1.43–44

> **What! was it you that would be England's king?**
> Was't you that revell'd in our parliament,
> **And made a preachment of your high descent?**
> **Where are your mess of sons to back you now?**
> **The wanton Edward, and the lusty George?**
> And where's that valiant crook-back prodigy,
> Dicky your boy, that with his grumbling voice
> **Was wont to cheer his dad in mutinies?**
> **Or, with the rest, where is your darling Rutland?**
>
> *Henry VI, Part 3*, 1.4.74–82

> **What's Montague?** it is nor hand, nor foot,
> Nor arm, nor face, nor any other part
> Belonging to a man. O, be some other name!
> **What's in a name?** that which we call a rose
> By any other name would smell as sweet;
> So Romeo would, were he not Romeo call'd,
> Retain that dear perfection which he owes
> Without that title. Romeo, doff thy name,
> And for that name which is no part of thee
> Take all myself.
>
> *Romeo and Juliet*, 2.2.42–51

What a piece of work is a man! how noble in reason! how
infinite in faculties! in form and moving how express and admirable! in action how like an angel! in apprehension how like a
god! The beauty of the world, the paragon of animals! **And yet
to me what is this quintessence of dust?**

Hamlet, 2.2.313–18

**If you prick us, do we not bleed? if you tickle us, do we not
laugh? if you poison us, do we not die?**

Merchant of Venice, 3.1.59–61

Simile

A simile is a rhetorical figure of speech comparing two unlike things,
usually using the words *like* or *as*.

True swains in love shall in the world to come
Approve their truths by Troilus: when their rhymes,
Full of protest, of oath and big compare,
Want similes, truth tired with iteration,
As true as steel, as plantage to the moon,
As sun to day, as turtle to her mate,
As iron to adamant, as earth to the centre,
Yet, after all comparisons of truth,
As truth's authentic author to be cited,
'As true as Troilus' shall crown up the verse,
And sanctify the numbers.

Troilus and Cressida, 3.2.175–85

They are **as gentle**
As zephyrs blowing below the violet,
Not wagging his sweet head; **and yet as rough,**
Their royal blood enchafed, as the rudest wind,
That by the top doth take the mountain pine,
And make him stoop to the vale.

Cymbeline, 4.2.226–31

His foes are so enrooted with his friends
That, plucking to unfix an enemy,
He doth unfasten so and shake a friend.
So that this land, **like an offensive wife**
That hath enrag'd him on to offer strokes,
As he is striking, holds his infant up,
And hangs resolv'd correction in the arm
That was uprear'd to execution.

Henry IV, Part 2, 4.1.213–20

Wordplay

Elizabethan audiences loved wordplay, and Shakespeare used it throughout all his plays to emphasize the meaning or for comic effect. You need to pick up the pitch on the matching words and play one against the other—make them work for you.

Wordplay in Verse

I say we must not
So stain our judgment, or corrupt our hope,
To prostitute our past-cure malady
To empirics, or to dissever so
Our great self and our credit, to esteem
A **senseless help** when **help past sense** we deem.

All's Well That Ends Well, 2.1.135–40

Wordplay in Prose

They say all lovers swear more **performance** than they are able and yet reserve an ability that they never **perform**, vowing more than the perfection of ten and discharging less than the tenth part of one. They that have the voice of lions and the act of hares, are they not monsters?

Troilus and Cressida, 3.2.87–92

Wordplay in Dialogue

In this excerpt from *The Two Gentlemen of Verona*, notice the word-play on *tale* and *tail*, and on *tied* and *tide*:

> PANTHINO. Launce, away, away, aboard! thy master is shipped
> and thou art to post after with oars. What's the matter? why
> weepest thou, man? Away, ass! You'll lose the **tide**, if you
> tarry any longer.
>
> LAUNCE. It is no matter if the **tied** were lost; for it is the
> unkindest **tied** that ever any man **tied**.
>
> PANTHINO. What's the unkindest **tide**?
>
> LAUNCE. Why, he that's **tied** here, Crab, my dog.
>
> PANTHINO. Tut, man, I mean thou'lt lose the flood, and, in losing
> the flood, lose thy voyage, and, in losing thy voyage, lose thy
> master, and, in losing thy master, lose thy service, and, in
> losing thy service,—Why dost thou stop my mouth?
>
> LAUNCE. For fear thou shouldst lose thy **tongue**.
>
> PANTHINO. Where should I lose my **tongue**?
>
> LAUNCE. In thy **tale**.
>
> PANTHINO. In thy **tail**!
>
> LAUNCE. Lose the **tide**, and the voyage, and the master, and the
> service, and the **tied**! Why, man, if the river were dry, I am
> able to fill it with my tears; if the wind were down, I could
> drive the boat with my sighs.
>
> *The Two Gentlemen of Verona*, 2.3.34–54

In the following excerpt from *Romeo and Juliet*, notice the word-play on the four words which sound alike but have different meanings:

> SAMPSON. Gregory, o' my word, we'll not carry **coals**.
>
> GREGORY. No, for then we should be **colliers**.
>
> SAMPSON. I mean, an we be in **choler**, we'll draw.
>
> GREGORY. Ay, while you live, draw your neck out o' the **collar**.
>
> *Romeo and Juliet*, 1.1.1–4

Notice here how Shakespeare shifts the stress on *quickly*, *moved*, and *strike*:

> SAMPSON. I strike **quickly**, being **moved**.
> GREGORY. But thou art not **quickly moved** to **strike**.
>> *Romeo and Juliet*, 1.1.5–6

Wordplay in Rhyming Couplets

Wordplay is even used in rhyming couplets:

> But **know I think** and **think I know** most sure
> My art is not past power nor you past cure.
>> *All's Well That Ends Well*, 2.1.173–74

Complex Wordplay

Wordplay can go on for three or more lines:

> **Grace** me no **grace**, nor **uncle** me no **uncle**:
> I am no traitor's **uncle**; and that word **'grace.'**
> In an **ungracious** mouth is but profane.
>> *Richard II*, 2.3.91–93

> One woman is fair, yet I am well; another is wise, yet I am well; another virtuous, yet I am well; **but till all graces be in one woman, one woman shall not come in my grace**.
>> *Much Ado about Nothing*, 2.3.25–29

Wordplay and Shakespeare's Pronunciation

Elizabethan pronunciation differed significantly from our own. Vowels were in the process of changing, in a process known as a *vowel shift*—which is the same process that has given us so many different accents today. There are a number of words in Shakespeare's plays that would have made perfect rhymes then but now sound like half-rhymes: *love* and *prove*, for example.

In *Henry IV, Part 1,* Falstaff tells Hal, seemingly inexplicably:

> If **reasons** were as plentiful as blackberries, I would give no man a **reason** upon compulsion, I.
>> *Henry IV, Part 1*, 2.4.238–40

There is a pun here, but the modern audience would be hard-pressed to notice it, unless *reason* were pronounced in the Elizabethan manner, which would sound something like *raisin*. The pun then becomes obvious, and the line makes much more sense.

In *Julius Caesar*, Cassius puns on *Rome* and *room*—and again the words were pronounced alike in Shakespeare's time.

> Now is it **Rome** indeed and **room** enough,
> When there is in it but one only man.
>
> *Julius Caesar*, 1.2.165–66

Wordplay and Vocal Virtuosity

Elizabethan audiences loved vocal virtuosity and complex language. In *As You Like It*, the court jester Touchstone uses wordplay to demonstrate his ability with vocal virtuosity. The number seven had a special rhetorical flourish, as in the seven seas, the seven days of the week, and the miracle of the five loaves plus two fishes (thus a seven) in the Bible. The actor who played Touchstone was probably able to match the rhetorical with the physical gesture for each of the seven causes.

> TOUCHSTONE. Faith, we met, and found the quarrel was upon the **seventh** cause.
> JAQUES. How **seventh** cause? Good my lord, like this fellow.
> DUKE. I like him very well.
> TOUCHSTONE. God 'ild you, sir; I desire you of the like. I press in here, sir, amongst the rest of the country copulatives, to swear and to forswear, according as marriage binds and blood breaks. A poor virgin, sir, an ill-favour'd thing, sir, but mine own; a poor humour of mine, sir, to take that that man else will. Rich honesty dwells like a miser, sir, in a poor house; as your pearl in your foul oyster.
> DUKE. By my faith, he is very swift and sententious.
> TOUCHSTONE. According to the fool's bolt, sir, and such dulcet diseases.
> JAQUES. But, for the **seventh** cause: how did you find the quarrel on the **seventh** cause?

TOUCHSTONE. Upon a lie **seven times** removed—bear your body more seeming, Audrey—as thus, sir. I did dislike the cut of a certain courtier's beard; he sent me word, if I said his beard was not cut well, he was in the mind it was. This is call'd the Retort Courteous. If I sent him word again it was not well cut, he would send me word he cut it to please himself. This is call'd the Quip Modest. If again it was not well cut, he disabled my judgment. This is call'd the Reply Churlish. If again it was not well cut, he would answer I spake not true. This is call'd the Reproof Valiant. If again it was not well cut, he would say I lie. This is call'd the Countercheck Quarrelsome. And so to the Lie Circumstantial and the Lie Direct.

JAQUES. And how oft did you say his beard was not well cut?

TOUCHSTONE. I durst go no further than the Lie Circumstantial, nor he durst not give me the Lie Direct; and so we measur'd swords and parted.

JAQUES. Can you nominate in order now the degrees of the lie?

TOUCHSTONE. O, sir, we quarrel in print by the book, as you have books for good manners. I will name you the degrees. The first, the Retort Courteous; the second, the Quip Modest; the third, the Reply Churlish; the fourth, the Reproof Valiant; the fifth, the Countercheck Quarrelsome; the sixth, the Lie with Circumstance; **the seventh**, the Lie Direct. All these you may avoid but the Lie Direct; and you may avoid that too with an If. I knew when **seven justices** could not take up a quarrel; but when the parties were met themselves, one of them thought but of an If, as: 'If you said so, then I said so.' And they shook hands, and swore brothers. Your If is the only peace-maker; much virtue in If.

As You Like It, 5.4.50–93

In *Love's Labour's Lost*, Moth, the young servant to the pedant Don Armado, uses fantastical rhetoric to make fun of his master:

No, my complete master: but to jig off a tune at the tongue's end, canary to it with your feet, humour it with turning up your eyelids, sigh a note and sing a note, sometime through the throat, as if you swallowed love with singing love, sometime through the nose, as if you snuffed up love by smelling love; with your hat penthouse-like o'er the shop of your eyes; with your arms crossed on your thin-belly doublet like a rabbit on a spit; or your hands in your pocket like a man after the old painting; and keep not too long in one tune, but a snip and away. These are complements, these are humours; these betray nice wenches, that would be betrayed without these; and make them men of note—do you note me?—that most are affected to these.

Love's Labour's Lost, 3.1.9–23

Wordplay with Homophones

Shakespeare often uses similar sounding words as wordplay to emphasize the meaning in the text.

capitol/capital

> POLONIUS. I did enact Julius Caesar; I was kill'd i' th' **Capitol**; **Brutus** kill'd me.
> HAMLET. It was a **brute** part of him to kill so **capital** a calf there.
> *Hamlet*, 3.2.101–3

here/hear

> To her that is not **here**, nor doth not **hear**.
> *As You Like It*, 5.2.96

I/aye/eye

> say thou but '**I**,'
> And that bare vowel '**I**' shall poison more
> Than the death-darting **eye** of cockatrice:
> I am not I, if there be such an **I**;
> Or those eyes shut, that make thee answer '**I**.'
> If he be slain, say '**I**'; or if not, no:
> Brief sounds determine of my weal or woe.
> *Romeo and Juliet*, 3.2.48–54

whore/abhore

> I cannot say '**whore**:'
> It does **abhor** me now I speak the word;
>
> *Othello*, 4.2.193–94

whore/hoar

In this little jingle, the double meaning is in the identical sounds of "hoar," which means white frost but can also mean white hair, and "whore," which means a prostitute. A hare is also a euphemism for a prostitute. In medieval times, Pope Gregory I declared that baby rabbits could be considered fish and thus eaten during Lent. An old hare would not have been approved, however, so if a hare were baked into a Lenten pie, that pie would have to be eaten on the sly, which led to moldiness. Thus a prostitute who is too old and "spent" is too expensive and not worth the money.

> An old **hare hoar**
> And an old **hare hoar**
> Is very good meat in Lent;
> But a **hare** that is **hoar**
> Is too much for a score,
> When it **hoars** ere it be spent.
>
> *Romeo and Juliet*, 2.4.129–36

Wordplay with Puns

grave

> Ask for me to-morrow, and you shall find me a **grave** man.
> *Romeo and Juliet*, 3.1.103–4

tender (hold in regard, an offer, give)

> Think yourself a baby
> That you have ta'en these **tenders** for true pay,
> Which are not sterling. **Tender** yourself more dearly,
> Or (not to crack the wind of the poor phrase,
> Running it thus) you'll **tender** me a fool.
>
> *Hamlet*, 1.3.110–14

lethargy/lechery

> OLIVIA. Cousin, cousin, how have you come so early by this
> **lethargy**?
> SIR TOBY BELCH. Lechery! I defy **lechery**. There's one at the gate.
> *Twelfth Night*, 1.5.118–19

cousins/cozen'd

> **Cousins**, indeed; and by their uncle **cozen'd**
> Of comfort, kingdom, kindred, freedom, life.
> *Richard III*, 4.4.234–35

Other Uses of Language in Shakespeare's Plays

Although contemporary Shakespearean actors will benefit greatly
from an understanding of the principal rhetorical devices used in the
texts, they will also encounter other characteristics of Shakespeare's
language such as archaic words, French words, the pronunciation of
unfamiliar contractions, the use of stressed and unstressed syllables,
the difference in use between *thee/thou* and *you*, and at times some
large—and extremely unusual—words.

Archaic Words

Many words in Shakespeare's plays are archaic, meaning they are no
longer used in present-day English. Become familiar with them and
their pronunciation.

> *bade*—past tense of *bid*, pronounced like the current pronuncia-
> tion of *bad* (bæd)
> - She **bade** me to come in
> - I have laid those sheets you **bade** me on the bed.
> - My bloody judge **forbade** my tongue to speak;

This ring was mine; and, when I gave it Helen,
I **bade** her, if her fortunes ever stood
Necessitied to help, that by this token
I would relieve her.

All's Well That Ends Well, 5.3.95–98

When I did make thee free, sworest thou not then
To do this when I **bade** thee?

Antony and Cleopatra, 4.14.51–52

He hath commanded me to go to bed,
And **bade** me to dismiss you.

Othello, 4.3.13–14

dost (dust) dʌst dəst—archaic second person singular present of *to do*
- coward conscience, how **dost** thou afflict me!
- O, to what purpose **dost** thou hoard thy words,
- Thou frantic woman, what **dost** thou make here?

doth (duth) dʌθ, dəθ—archaic third person singular present of *to do*
- He **doth** bestride the narrow world like a colossus
- The lady **doth** protest too much methinks.
- Why should I not? **Doth** he not deserve well?

durst (derst) dɜːst—past tense and past participle of *to dare*
- These five days have I hid me in these woods and **durst** not peep out
- They **durst** not do 't;

ere (air) ɛə—before
- Meet me **ere** the first cock crow
- **Ere** they can hide their levity in honour;

Sirrah (sear uh) sɪrə—an extended form of *sir* used to express impatience to children or inferiors in rank
- Hold, **sirrah**, bear you these letters tightly.
- What, one good in ten? you corrupt the song, **sirrah**.
- What does this knave here? Get you gone, **sirrah**:

trow (trow) trō̄—to believe, suppose, know
- **Trow** you who hath done this?
- What is the matter, **trow**?
- 'Twas time, I **trow**, to wake and leave our beds,

Greetings
God gi'good e'en (God give good evening)
- God **gi'good e'en**; I pray, sir, can you read?

God-den (Good evening)
- **God-den** to your worships:
- **God-den**, good fellow.

God ye good-morrow
- **God ye good-morrow**, gentlemen

Expletives
By my holidame (By our holy dame, or Mary)
- Now, **by my holidame**. / What manner of man are you?
- Now, **by my holidame**, here comes Katherina!

By my troth (By my truth, or pledge)
- **By my troth**, I was seeking for a fool when I found you.
- **By my troth**, well met.

By'r lady (By our lady)
- Now, sirs: **by'r lady**, you fought fair;
- Ill news, **by'r lady**; seldom comes the better:

By'r lakin (By our lady-kin)
- **By'r lakin**, I can go no further, sir; My old bones ache.
- **By'r lakin**, a parlous fear.

Gramercies (Great thanks)
- **Gramercies**, Tranio, well dost thou advise.
- **Gramercies**, lad. Go forward; this contents;

'Sblood (God's blood)
- **'Sblood**, I am as melancholy / as a gib cat or a lugged bear.
- **'Sblood**, but you'll not hear me!

God's bodykins (By God's dear body)
- **God's bodykins**, man, much better!
- **Bodykins**, Master Page,

God-a-mercy
- Well, **God-a-mercy**
- **God-a-mercy**, old heart! thou speak'st cheerfully.

God 'ild and *Goddild (God yield)*
- **Goddild** you for your last company.
- How you shall bid **God 'ild** us for your pains,

Zounds (God's wounds)
- **Zounds**, where thou wilt, lad;
- **Zounds**, sir, you're robbed! For shame, put on your gown.

'Sdeath (God's death, pronounced with a *z* as *zdeath*)
- **'Sdeath**! The rabble should have first unroof'd the city, / Ere so prevail'd with me:
- and I know not—**'Sdeath**!

'Slight (God's light)
- **'Slight**, I could so beat the rogue!
- **'Slight**, will you make an ass o' me?

French Words

After the Norman Conquest in 1066, French became the language of the English nobility and was spoken at court. Although by Shakespeare's time English had supplanted French at court, French words were still in common use, but they were generally given anglicized pronunciation in his plays. I recommend that you consult a source such as Gary Logan's *The Eloquent Shakespeare* for the pronunciation of French words in Shakespeare's plays.[16]

adieu (ə'dju:)—He fumbles up into a loose **adieu**

Calais (kælɪs)—On toward **Calais**, ho!

Dauphin ('dɔfɪn)—We are glad the **Dauphin** is so pleasant with us;

Duke of Milan ('mɪlən)—Thy father was the **Duke of Milan**

Jacques (dʒeǐks)—My brother **Jacques** he keeps at school,

Jacques (dʒeǐkwi:z)—What you will Monsieur **Jacques**

liege ('li:dʒ)—My gracious sovereign, my most loving **liege**!

madame ('mædəm)—I, **madame**? No. I have no reason for it;

monsieur ('məsjɜ)—Good **monsieur** Charles, what's the new news at the new court

parle (pɑəl)—Of all the fair resort of gentlemen / that every day with **parle** encounter me.

puissance ('pwisəns)—And make imaginary **puissance**.

sans (sænz)—**sans** teeth, **sans** eyes, **sans** taste, **sans** everything.

Stressed Syllables

English is a language of stressed and unstressed syllables. The stressed syllables in Shakespeare's plays give the lines their rhythm and correct sense, enabling an audience to understand the meaning of the spoken text. This is true of both prose and iambic pentameter. Allow the pitch to rise slightly on stressed syllables rather than pressing down on the syllable or trying to make it louder.

- To be, or not to be: that is the question:
- Deny thy father and refuse thy name
- And every fair from fair sometime declines
- Make mad the guilty, and appall the free,

Changes in Meaning with Stress

Some words in English change stress depending on whether they are verbs or nouns. A shift in stress can change the entire definition of a word as well as the meter.

ábject/abjéct

- That he should be so ábject, base and poor,
- Let him that thinks of me so abjéctly
- Upon these paltry, servile, ábject drudges!

cómpound/compóunded
- Yea, this solidity and **cóm**pound mass,
- We have com**póund**ed on.
- Commanded of me those most poisonous **cóm**pounds,
- Com**póund**ed it with dust, whereto 'tis kin.

conténtc/cóntent
- A woman sometimes scorns what best con**ténts** her
- I know not the **cón**tents;
- Pray you, con**tént** you
- And for the **cón**tents' sake are sorry for our pain.

contráct/cóntract
- I have no joy in this con**tráct** tonight.
- Good fortune and the favour of the king Smile upon this **cón**tract;
- To be con**tráct**ed in one brow of woe,
- The **cón**tract you pretend with that base wretch,
- Here are the articles of con**tráct**ed peace

cónvert/convért
- But Harry lives that shall con**vért** those tears
- He thence departs a heavy **cón**vertite;
- May I be so con**vért**ed and see with these eyes?

desért/désert—don't confuse this word with *dessert*, a sweet dish at the end of a meal. It means "deserving" or an arid piece of land.
- Yet never know how that de**sért** should be.
- You less know how to value her de**sért**
- Being native burghers of this **dé**sert city
- 'Why should this a **dé**sert be?

divérsely/dívers (different)
- but that our wits are so di**vérse**ly coloured:
- Time travels in **dí**vers paces with **dí**vers persons.
- Myself and **dí**vers gentlemen beside

ínjury/injúrious
- I do protest I never **ín**jured thee
- In**júr**ious wasps, to feed on such sweet honey
- It were for me / To throw my sceptre at the in**júr**ious gods;
- God! they did me too much **ín**jury

óbject/objéct
- The **ób**ject of art is to give life a shape.
- And mark what **ób**ject did present itself.
- He doth ob**jéct** I am too great of birth—,
- what dost thou ob**jéct** / Against the Duke of Norfolk,

pérfect/perféct
- Ere I can per**féct** mine intents, to kneel:
- So holy and so **pér**fect is my love,
- That she did make de**féct** per**féct**ion,
- and thy most **pér**fect goodness

réfuge/refúge
- I did imagine what would be her **ré**fuge
- beggars who sitting in the stocks re**fúge** their shame, that others must sit there.
- Well, I will for **ré**fuge straight to Bristol castle:

réfuse/refúse
- Deny thy father and re**fúse** they name
- teeming **ré**fuse
- But if you do re**fúse** to marry me,
- That in the very **ré**fuse of thy deeds

revénue/révenue
- If I would lose it for a **ré**venue
- She bears a duke's re**vé**nues on her back.
- Long withering out a young man **ré**venue.
- To have th' expense and waste of his re**vé**nues.

súbject/subjéct

- Subjécted thus / How can you say to me I am a king?
- How many thousand of my poorest **súb**jects
- For he himself is **súb**ject to his birth
- I rather will subjéct me to the malice / Of a diverted blood and bloody brother.

whóre/abhóre

- O, though I love what others do abhór,
- With others thou shouldst not abhór my state.
- Thou **whóre**son, senseless villain!
- I cannot say "**whóre**": It does abhór me now I speak the word;

Practice Selection for Stressed Syllables and Meaning

I have heard
The cock, that is the trumpet to the morn,
Doth with his lofty and shrill-sounding throat
Awake the god of day; and at his warning,
Whether in sea or fire, in earth or air,
Th' extravagant and erring spirit hies
To his confíne; and of the truth herein
This present **ób**ject made probation.

Hamlet, 1.1.172–79

Contractions

When using contractions of words in Shakespeare, don't add another syllable to the word. For example, when saying "And **wouldst** thou have me cast my love on him?" don't pronounce "wouldst" as "would-est."

- **Will't** please your lordship cool your hands?'
- Thou **did'st** it excellent.
- What **is't** your honour will command?
- I **ne'er** drank sak in my life.
- "What **think'st** thou

- The trick **of's** frown; his forehead;
- The milk thou **suck'dst** from her did turn to marble;
- When in eternal lines to time thou **grow'st**:
- That wishing well had not a body **in't**
- But my intents are **fix'd** and will not leave me.
- I will as **'twere** a brother of your order.
- But now I am **cabin'd**, **cribbb'd**, **confin'd**,
- I drink to the general joy **o' th'** whole table
- Ay me! but yet thou **mightst** my seat forbear
- till he hath **ta'en** thy life by some indirect means or other
- By wondering how thou **took'st** it.
- My do **t'express** his love and friendling to you
- Let us withdraw; **'twill** be a storm
- what beast **w'ast** then
- Let her **know't**.

Inflection

Inflection is the rise, fall, and change in pitch of modulation in the voice that indicates a change in meaning or intention.

Let the inflection rise until the thought is complete—usually at a period, when the voice drops down, completing the thought.

> Now entertain conjecture of a time ↑
> When creeping murmur and the poring dark ↑
> Fills the wide vessel of the universe. ↓
>
> *Henry V, Part 4*, prologue.1–3

> Gallop apace, ↑ you fiery-footed steeds, ↑
> Towards Phoebus' lodging: ↑ such a wagoner
> As Phaethon would whip you to the west, ↑
> And bring in cloudy night immediately. ↓
>
> *Romeo and Juliet*, 3.2.1–4

Operative Words

An operative word is simply a word that is stressed.
- These are the forgeries of **jealousy**
- Maybe she doth but **counterfeit**

Emphasize the word that carries the meaning by lifting it or the stressed syllable in pitch.

> Your **If**, is the only peace-maker: much virtue in **If**.
>
> *As You Like It*, 5.4.93

> BASSANIO. If you did know to **whom** I gave the ring,
>   If you did know **for** whom I gave the ring
>   And would conceive for **what** I gave the ring
>   And how unwillingly I **left** the ring,
>   When nought would be accepted **but** the ring,
>   You would **abate** the strength of your displeasure.
> PORTIA. If you had known the **virtue** of the ring,
>   Or half her worthiness that **gave** the ring,
>   Or your own honour to **contain** the ring,
>   You would not then have **parted** with the ring.
>
> *The Merchant of Venice*, 5.1.217–26

> My lord, your son was **gone** before I **came**.
>
> *Richard II*, 2.2.990

Personal Pronouns

Only stress personal pronouns if you are making a comparison as an argument.

> Alas, poor fool! why do I pity **him**
> That with his very heart despiseth **me**?
>
> *Two Gentlemen of Verona*, 4.4.98–99

> If that be sin, I'll make it my morn prayer
> To have it added to the faults of **mine**,
> And nothing of **your** answer.
>
> *Measure for Measure*, 2.4.80–82

> What should it be that **he** respects in **her**
> But **I** can make respective in **myself**,
>
> *Two Gentlemen of Verona*, 4.4.201–2

Thou, Thee, Thy, Thine / You, Ye, Your, Yours

According to British linguist David Crystal, the difference in use of these words derived from the *tu/vous* usage in French: "*Thou* was originally used for addressing one person, and *ye/you* for more than one. But during [Shakespeare's time], usage changed: *thou* became intimate and informal, and *ye/you* polite and respectful."[17] He elaborates that this distinction "did sometimes indicate social class, as with Toby Belch's 'if thou thou'st him some thrice . . .'. But more often it expressed a difference in the relationship between characters, as when Hamlet *thou*s Ophelia ('Get thee to a nunnery') and the like. The switch alters the atmosphere or temperature (or whatever metaphor you like to use) of a relationship."[18] The pronunciation of these words is not an issue. It's just something an actor might want to think about when working on the text.

In this scene from *As You Like It*, Celia and Rosalind, who are cousins (daughter and niece of the ruling Duke Frederick), use both *thee* and *you* in the same scene:

> CELIA. I pray **thee**, Rosalind, sweet my coz, be merry.
>
> ROSALIND. Dear Celia, I show more mirth than I am mistress of; and would **you** yet I were merrier? Unless **you** could teach me to forget a banished father, **you** must not learn me how to remember any extraordinary pleasure.
>
> CELIA. Herein I see **thou** lov'st me not with the full weight that I love **thee**. If my uncle, **thy** banished father, had banished **thy** uncle, the Duke my father, so **thou** hadst been still with me, I could have taught my love to take **thy** father for mine; so wouldst **thou**, if the truth of **thy** love to me were so righteously temper'd as mine is to **thee**.
>
> ROSALIND. Well, I will forget the condition of **my** estate, to rejoice in **yours**.
>
> *As You Like It*, 1.2.1–13

This is just another way of looking at choices an actor might consider and could be a subject for discussion in the rehearsal room. In terms of the relationship between Rosalind and Celia, there really isn't a class difference between the two of them.

Large Words

When encountering large words in Shakespeare, sound them out, use the principle of repetition, and theatricalize it.

- Ah me, most **credulous** fool! / **Egregious** murderer
- The princes **orgulous**, their high blood chafed
- a **gallimaufry** of gambols
- he'll speak like an **Anthropophaganian**
- the **multidudinous** seas **incarnadine**
- **Videlicet** in a love cause
- The **cognizance** of **her incontinency**

> O, they have lived long on the alms-basket of words. I marvel thy master hath not eaten thee for a word; for thou art not so long by the head as **honorificabilitudinitatibus**: thou art easier swallowed than a flap-dragon.
>
> *Love's Labour's Lost*, 5.1.40–44

5

Shakespeare's Use of Verse and Prose

Shakespeare wrote his plays using both verse and prose. When looking at the text of his plays, it is easy to see which is which. Each line of verse follows a five-beat pattern, with the beginning of each new line capitalized. Prose, on the other hand, runs across the page or column until the end of the paragraph, with no special capitalization from line to line. Here are two examples from *As You Like It* in which the same characters, Rosalind and Celia, speak in prose in the first and in verse in the second:

CELIA. I pray thee, Rosalind, sweet my coz, be merry.
ROSALIND. Dear Celia, I show more mirth than I am mistress of;
    and would you yet I were merrier? Unless you could teach
    me to forget a banished father, you must not learn me how
    to remember any extraordinary pleasure.

As You Like It, 1.2.1–5

ROSALIND. Why, whither shall we go?
CELIA. To seek my uncle in the Forest of Arden.
ROSALIND. Alas, what danger will it be to us,
    Maids as we are, to travel forth so far!
    Beauty provoketh thieves sooner than gold.

CELIA. I'll put myself in poor and mean attire,
    And with a kind of umber smirch my face;
    The like do you; so shall we pass along,
    And never stir assailants.

As You Like It, 1.3.105–13

The reasons why Shakespeare writes in verse and why he writes in prose are complex and in some cases impossible to know for sure, but these are important considerations for an actor.

Iambic Pentameter or Blank Verse

The cornerstone of verse speaking is the meter—it is the pulse that drives the text forward. What determines the meter are the stressed syllables in a line of verse. (These are sometimes referred to as accented and unaccented syllables, but for clarity they will now be referred to only as stressed and unstressed syllables.)

In Shakespeare's text, when he is writing in verse, the text generally consists of a five-stressed-syllable line called *iambic pentameter* (*penta* means "five"; *meter* means "length"). An *iamb* is a metrical foot of two syllables: an unstressed syllable followed by a stressed syllable. A *pentameter* is a verse line of five metrical feet. In England iambic pentameter is more commonly called *blank verse*. It is also the basic rhythm of the English language and is found in everyday English speech, as in "I asked for water, but they brought me beer."

In its strictest sense, iambic pentameter is a line of verse consisting of ten syllables, having the second, fourth, sixth, eighth, and tenth stressed, and the others unstressed:

- And évery fáir from fáir sometíme declínes,
- My bónds in thée are áll detérminate
- Of áll the wónders thát I yét have séen,

Break in the Iambic Verse Line

In practice, however, there is much variation in Shakespeare's writing; otherwise, the monotony of the form would defeat its purpose. Notice that in the first line of Sonnet 29, the stress is on the first word, "When":

Whén, in disgráce with fórtune and mén's éyes,

The break in the pattern catches the ear and makes the listener aware of a shift in meaning. Here are some other examples in which the stress is on the first syllable:

- Gállop apáce, you fíery-fóoted stéeds,
- Hóod my únmanned blóod, báting in my chéeks
- Stánd in the plágue of cústom ánd permít

You will notice that the last two lines are not regular and contain some one-syllable words, or monosyllables, which allow for choices on which word gets the most stress. What drives the line is the lift in pitch on the *stressed* syllables. Also, when there is an extra unstressed syllable in a line, giving the line eleven syllables instead of ten, the line is said to have a *feminine ending*. The eleventh syllable is weak and is not stressed.

- To bé or nót to bé—that ís the quéstion
- A wóman móved is líke a fóuntain tróubled
- Farewéll—thou árt too déar for mý posséssing,

Whether an ending to a line is feminine or not should not make any difference in the way the word is pronounced. An audience shouldn't be suddenly confronted by an unusual pronunciation of the end of a line of verse just to stress an extra syllable such as: Swílled with the wíld and wásteful óceán (oh shee un). There are differing opinions about the effect of a feminine ending on the meaning of a line. Some directors think it is significant, so I am including this explanation. No actor should be blindsided by a feminine ending.

Rhyming Couplets

Rhyming couplets are two rhyming lines written in iambic pentameter. The rhyme is part of the meaning and can't be ignored; however, it is not necessary to overemphasize the rhyme. Just make sure you don't let the voice land with a thud on the last syllable.

> My only love sprung from my only **hate**!
> Too early seen unknown, and known too **late**!
> *Romeo and Juliet*, 1.5.159–60

> But know I think and think I know most **sure**
> My art is not past power nor you past **cure**.
> *All's Well That Ends Well*, 2.1.173–74

> Prodigious birth of love it is to **me**,
> That I must love a loathed **enemy**.
> *Romeo and Juliet*, 1.5.151–52

In *All's Well That Ends Well*, Helena, the young ward of the Countess of Rousillon, is in love with the Countess's son Bertram, who does not return her love. In this soliloquy, Helena ponders whether her fate, which is believed to be written in the stars, can be overcome by will and action. It is written in rhymed couplets, but try to stay off the rhyme and focus on what she is trying to say:

> Our remedies oft in ourselves do lie,
> Which we ascribe to heaven: the fated sky
> Gives us free scope, only doth backward pull
> Our slow designs when we ourselves are dull.
> What power is it which mounts my love so high,
> That makes me see, and cannot feed mine eye?
> The mightiest space in fortune nature brings
> To join like likes and kiss like native things.
> Impossible be strange attempts to those
> That weigh their pains in sense and do suppose
> What hath been cannot be: who ever strove

So show her merit, that did miss her love?
The king's disease—my project may deceive me,
But my intents are fix'd and will not leave me. *Exit*
All's Well That Ends Well, 1.1.218–31

I don't suggest that these are the only stresses possible in this speech, but the stressed syllables and operative words are what helps the actor make sense of the text. The rhyme is there, but it does not overwhelm the sense.

In this example from *A Midsummer Night's Dream*, Helena's dialogue is in rhyming couplets. It would create a kind of "sing-song" to accent the rhyme, so again it is better to stress the words that express the sense of the line:

How happy some o'er other some can be!
Through Athens **I** am thought as fair as **she**.
But what of that? **Demetrius** thinks not so;
He will **not** know what all but he **do** know:
And as **he** errs, doting on Hermia's eyes,
So **I**, admiring of his qualities:
A Midsummer Night's Dream, 1.1.237–42
(note that *eyes* and *qualities* once rhymed)

Rhyming Couplets that End a Scene

When a rhyming couplet ends a scene, it is generally used as a device to get the characters offstage with a flourish as the next scene begins. Make sure you use the couplet in that way and play the rhyme.

Come home with me to supper; and I'll **lay**
A plot shall show us all a merry **day**.
Richard II, 4.1.348–49

And when I have my meed, I must **away**;
For this will out, and here I must not **stay**.
Richard III, 1.4.283–84

Be gone to-morrow; and be sure of **this**,
What I can help thee to thou shalt not **miss**.
All's Well That Ends Well, 1.3.263–64

Flourish. Exeunt

Sometimes a rhymed couplet is used to punctuate the end of the play:

> For never was a story of more **woe**
> Than this of Juliet and her **Romeo**.
> > *Romeo and Juliet*, 5.3.351–52

> The oldest have borne most; we that are **young**
> Shall never see so much, nor live so **long**.
> > *King Lear*, 5.3.395–96

> Till then I'll sweat and seek about for **eases**,
> And at that time bequeath you my **diseases**.
> > *Troilus and Cressida*, 5.10.59–60

Rhyming Couplets in Dialogue

When there are rhyming couplets in dialogue, emphasize the operative words rather the stressing the rhyme.

> FERDINAND. Your oath is pass'd to pass away from **these**.
> BIRON. Let me say no, my liege, an if you **please**:
> > I only swore to study with your **grace**
> > And stay here in your court for three years' **space**.
> LONGAVILLE. You swore to that, Biron, and to the **rest**.
> BIRON. By yea and nay, sir, then I swore in **jest**.
> > What is the end of study? let me know.
> FERDINAND. Why, that to know, which else we should not know.
> BIRON. Things hid and barr'd, you mean, from common **sense**?
> FERDINAND. Ay, that is study's godlike **recompense**.
> > *Love's Labour's Lost*, 1.1.51–60

> FERDINAND. Madam, I will, if suddenly I **may**.
> PRINCESS OF FRANCE. You will the sooner, that I were **away**;
> > For you'll prove perjured if you make me **stay**.
> > *Love's Labour Lost*, 2.1.115–17

Trochee

A *trochee* is a stressed syllable followed by an unstressed syllable. Often, Shakespeare will choose a word with the stress on the first syllable, which alerts the ear of the listener because it breaks the regular line, while the rest of the line continues in iambic pentameter.

- Angels and ministers of grace defend us
- Sleep shall neither night nor day
- Swifter than the moon's sphere

Rarely, a trochaic line can also be pentameter, as in this line from *King Lear*:

> Never, never, never, never, never!

Actors don't need to worry about trochee—the stress automatically falls on the first syllable of the word because that is how it is usually pronounced. However, since some directors might mention it, I'm including it here.

Rhymed Tetrameter Couplets

Shakespeare will often switch from iambic pentameter to *trochaic tetrameter*, which has four trochees, felt as four beats, to a line. It appears especially in songs or in chants, such as the one the witches in *Macbeth* recite multiple times in act 4, scene 1:

> Double, double toil and trouble;
> Fire burn and caldron bubble.

Some of the last words of the lines in the following excerpt from *A Midsummer Night's Dream* rhymed in Shakespeare's time, but no longer do in modern English. For example, "remedy" was pronounced as "re-muh-dye" and rhymed with "by." If a production is using Original Pronunciation, that would be the way to pronounce those words, otherwise just use modern pronunciation:

PUCK. Through the forest have I **gone**.
    But Athenian found I **none**,
    On whose eyes I might approve
    This flower's force in stirring love.
    Night and silence.—Who is **here**?
    Weeds of Athens he doth **wear**:
    This is he, my master said,
    Despised the Athenian maid;
    And here the maiden, sleeping **sound**,
    On the dank and dirty **ground**.
                         A Midsummer Night's Dream, 2.2.72–81

OBERON. Flower of this purple **dye**,
    Hit with Cupid's archery,
    Sink in apple of his **eye**.
    When his love he doth **espy**,
    Let her shine as gloriously
    As the Venus of the **sky**.
    When thou wakest, if she be **by**,
    Beg of her for **remedy**.
PUCK. Captain of our fairy **band**,
    Helena is here at **hand**;
    And the youth, mistook by **me**,
    Pleading for a lover's **fee**.
    Shall we their fond pageant **see**?
    Lord, what fools these mortals **be**!
                         A Midsummer Night's Dream, 3.2.109–23

Sometimes the language in a scene can change meters, as in this scene from *King Lear*. During a storm, Lear, Kent, and the Fool find shelter with Edgar, who is disguised as Poor Tom, a madman. Edgar's speech changes from iambic pentameter to trochee and then to prose as he tries to comfort Lear by confronting the imaginary dogs that seem to threaten him, while at the same time still giving the impression that he himself is mad:

EDGAR. [*aside*] My tears begin to take his part so much
  They'll mar my counterfeiting.
LEAR. The little dogs and all,
  Tray, Blanch and Sweetheart, see, they bark at me.
EDGAR. Tom will throw his head at them. Avaunt, you curs!
  Be thy mouth or black or white,
  Tooth that poisons if it bite;
  Mastiff, greyhound, mongrel grim,
  Hound or spaniel, brach or lym,
  Bobtail tyke or trundle-tail—
  Tom will make them weep and wail;
  For, with throwing thus my head,
  Dogs leap the hatch, and all are fled.
  Do de, de, de. Sessa! Come, march to wakes and fairs and
  market-towns. Poor Tom, thy horn is dry.

                                              King Lear, 3.6.55–69

Individual trochees also appear as irregularities in lines that are
otherwise iambic. In *Twelfth Night*, Feste, who is Lady Olivia's fool,
sings what was an old song during Shakespeare's time when he visits
Malvolio, who is imprisoned under suspicion of madness:

FESTE. Nay, I'll ne'er believe a madman till I see his brains.
  I will fetch you light and paper and ink.
MALVOLIO. Fool, I'll requite it in the highest degree: I prithee,
  be gone.
FESTE. I am gone, sir,
  And anon, sir,
  I'll be with you again,
  In a trice,
  Like to the old Vice,
  Your need to sustain;
  Who, with dagger of lath,
  In his rage and his wrath,
  Cries, ah, ha! to the devil:
  Like a mad lad,
  Pare thy nails, dad;
  Adieu, good man devil.

                                        Twelfth Night, 4.2.111–27

Alliteration and Meter

The syllables can also be driven by alliteration, so be aware of the beat on the repeated consonants:

> O gentle **P**andarus,
> From Cu**p**id's shoulder **p**luck his **p**ainted wings
> And fly with me to Cressid!
>
> *Troilus and Cressida*, 3.2.13–15

> A **f**ool, a **f**ool! I met a **f**ool i' th' **f**orest,
> A **m**otley **f**ool. A **m**iserable world!
> As I do live by **f**ood, I met a **f**ool,
> Who laid him down and bask'd him in the sun,
> And rail'd on Lady **F**ortune in good terms,
> In good set terms—and yet a **m**otley **f**ool.
>
> *As You Like It*, 2.7.12–17

> That **t**ongue that **t**ells the story of thy days,
>
> Sonnet 95.5

Shared Lines

With shared lines, be sure to pick up cues—don't pause. A shared line is always spontaneous because changing a thought in the middle of a verse line drives the scene forward.

> OTHELLO. I crave fit disposition for my wife.
>   Due reference of place and exhibition,
>   With such accommodation and besort
>   As levels with her breeding.
> DUKE.   If you please,
>   Be't at her father's.
> BRABANTIO.   I'll not have it so.
> OTHELLO. Nor I.
> DESDEMONA. Nor I; I would not there reside,
>   To put my father in impatient thoughts
>   By being in his eye. Most gracious duke,
>   To my unfolding lend your prosperous ear;

And let me find a charter in your voice,
To assist my simpleness.

DUKE. What would you, Desdemona?

Othello, 1.3.258–72

Shakespeare's Prose

Shakespeare's characters switch from verse to prose and vice versa, frequently in the same scene. An actor should be aware of when his or her character switches from verse to prose or from prose to verse and consider why. Prose is just as demanding to speak as verse, in some cases more so.

Verse is easier to remember, because the words make a pattern on the page while resembling ordinary speech. It can also express heightened emotion and deep feelings. In this scene from *Hamlet*, Ophelia attempts to return Hamlet's gifts and he confronts her for not being honest with him. Note that he speaks in prose, and when he exits, she replies in verse:

HAMLET. Ha, ha! Are you honest?

OPHELIA. My lord?

HAMLET. Are you fair?

OPHELIA. What means your lordship?

HAMLET. That if you be honest and fair, your honesty should admit no discourse to your beauty.

OPHELIA. Could beauty, my lord, have better commerce than with honesty?

HAMLET. Ay, truly; for the power of beauty will sooner transform honesty from what it is to a bawd than the force of honesty can translate beauty into his likeness. This was sometime a paradox, but now the time gives it proof. I did love you once.

OPHELIA. Indeed, my lord, you made me believe so.

HAMLET. You should not have believ'd me; for virtue cannot so inoculate our old stock but we shall relish of it. I loved you not.

OPHELIA. I was the more deceived.

HAMLET. Get thee to a nunnery! Why wouldst thou be a breeder of sinners? I am myself indifferent honest, but yet I could accuse me of such things that it were better my mother had not borne me. I am very proud, revengeful, ambitious; with more offences at my beck than I have thoughts to put them in, imagination to give them shape, or time to act them in. What should such fellows as I do, crawling between earth and heaven? We are arrant knaves all; believe none of us. Go thy ways to a nunnery. Where's your father?

OPHELIA. At home, my lord.

HAMLET. Let the doors be shut upon him, that he may play the fool nowhere but in's own house. Farewell.

OPHELIA. O, help him, you sweet heavens!

HAMLET. If thou dost marry, I'll give thee this plague for thy dowry: be thou as chaste as ice, as pure as snow, thou shalt not escape calumny. Get thee to a nunnery. Go, farewell. Or if thou wilt needs marry, marry a fool; for wise men know well enough what monsters you make of them. To a nunnery, go; and quickly too. Farewell.

OPHELIA. O heavenly powers, restore him!

HAMLET. I have heard of your paintings too, well enough. God hath given you one face, and you make yourselves another. You jig, you amble, and you lisp; you nickname God's creatures and make your wantonness your ignorance. Go to, I'll no more on't! it hath made me mad. I say, we will have no more marriages. Those that are married already— all but one—shall live; the rest shall keep as they are. To a nunnery, go.

OPHELIA. O, what a noble mind is here o'erthrown!
The courtier's, scholar's, soldier's, eye, tongue, sword,
Th' expectancy and rose of the fair state,
The glass of fashion and the mould of form,
Th' observ'd of all observers—quite, quite down!
And I, of ladies most deject and wretched,
That suck'd the honey of his music vows,
Now see that noble and most sovereign reason,
Like sweet bells jangled, out of tune and harsh;
That unmatch'd form and feature of blown youth

Blasted with ecstasy. O, woe is me
T' have seen what I have seen, see what I see!

Hamlet, 3.1.101–59

In Shakespeare's plays, prose is often spoken by characters who are of lower status, such as servants or peasants. In *The Winter's Tale* an Old Shepherd complains to the audience in prose about his lost sheep and then discovers the castaway baby, Perdita:

> I would there were no age between sixteen and three-and-twenty, or that youth would sleep out the rest; for there is nothing in the between but getting wenches with child, wronging the ancientry, stealing, fighting—Hark you now! Would any but these boiled brains of nineteen and two-and-twenty hunt this weather? They have scared away two of my best sheep, which I fear the wolf will sooner find than the master: if any where I have them, 'tis by the seaside, browsing of ivy. Good luck, an't be thy will what have we here! Mercy on 's, a barne a very pretty barne! A boy or a child, I wonder? A pretty one; a very pretty one: sure, some 'scape: though I am not bookish, yet I can read waiting-gentlewoman in the 'scape. This has been some stair-work, some trunk-work, some behind-door-work: they were warmer that got this than the poor thing is here. I'll take it up for pity: yet I'll tarry till my son come; he hallooed but even now. Whoa, ho, hoa!

The Winter's Tale, 3.3.66–85

Peter, the household servant of the Capulets in *Romeo and Juliet*, speaks in prose that is full of mixed metaphors, which points up his attempts to emulate his betters despite his lack of formal education.

> Find them out whose names are written here! It is written, that the shoemaker should meddle with his yard, and the tailor with his last, the fisher with his pencil, and the painter with his nets; but I am sent to find those persons whose names are here writ, and can never find what names the writing person hath here writ. I must to the learned.—In good time.

Romeo and Juliet, 1.2.40–46

In contrast, Romeo's speech at his death is expressed in verse:

> O, here
> Will I set up my everlasting rest,
> And shake the yoke of inauspicious stars
> From this world-wearied flesh. Eyes, look your last!
>
> *Romeo and Juliet*, 5.3.121–24

Yet, Hamlet's speech on the subject of death toward the end of *Hamlet*, while heightened, is in prose, so status is not always indicative.

> Not a whit, we defy augury; there's a special providence in the fall of a sparrow. If it be now, 'tis not to come; if it be not to come, it will be now; if it be not now, yet it will come: the readiness is all. Since no man knows aught of what he leaves, what is't to leave betimes?
>
> *Hamlet*, 5.2.203–7

Stressed Syllables in Prose

Even in prose, English is a language of stressed and unstressed syllables. The pitch lifts slightly on the stressed syllable, enabling us to understand the meaning of the word. This is true whether Shakespeare's text is in prose or in iambic pentameter. Let the pitch rise slightly on stressed syllables rather than pressing down on the syllable or just trying to make it louder.

Rhetorical Figures in Prose

Shakespeare's prose uses all the rhetorical figures attributed to verse except meter, and even there, the stressed syllables of the words create a rhythm that drives the text.

Notice the alliteration and antithesis in the following speech of Rosalind's from *As You Like It*:

Dear Celia, I show **more mirth** than I am **mistress** of; and would you yet I were **merrier**? Unless you could **teach** me to **forget** a banished father, you must not **learn** me how to **remember** any extraordinary pleasure.

As You Like It, 1.2.2–5

Prose can show the state of a character and the character's emotional change, as this speech of Mercutio's from *Romeo and Juliet*, which again uses alliteration and assonance, makes clear:

Alas poor Romeo! He is already dead; stabbed with a white wench's black eye; shot through the ear with a love-song; the very pin of his heart cleft with the **blind bow-boy's butt-**shaft: and is he a **man** to encounter Tybalt?

Romeo and Juliet, 2.4.12–16

Look at Rosalind's epilogue from *As You Like It*, and note the rhetorical devices that Shakespeare gives the character of Rosalind:

It is not the **fashion** to see the **lady** the **epilogue**; but it is no more **unhandsome** than to see the **lord** the **prologue** [triple antithesis]. If it be true that **good wine needs no bush**, 'tis true that a **good play needs no epilogue** [antithesis]. Yet to good wine they do use good bushes; and good plays prove the better by the help of good epilogues. What a case am I in then, that am neither a good epilogue, nor cannot insinuate with you in the behalf of a good play! I am not furnish'd like a **beggar**; therefore to **beg** will not **become me** [alliteration and word-play]. My way is to conjure you; and I'll begin with the women. I charge you, **O women, for the love you bear to men,** to like as much of this play as please you; and I charge you, **O men, for the love you bear to women** [antithesis]—as I perceive by your simp'ring none of you hates them—that between you and the women the play may please. If I were a woman, I would kiss as many of you as had beards that pleas'd me, complexions that lik'd me, and breaths that I defied not; and, I am sure, as many as have good beards, or good faces, or sweet breaths, will, for my kind offer, when I make curtsy, bid me farewell.

As You Like It, 5.4.194–211

In the following monologue and lead-in, written in prose, Hamlet questions his former schoolmates Rosencrantz and Guildenstern as to whether they were sent for by the King and Queen to visit him in Elsinore. When they finally confess that they have been sent for, Hamlet uses heightened language with soaring metaphors to explain his frame of mind to them. The speech could easily be taken for verse by a listening audience, yet it is in prose:

> HAMLET. That you must teach me. But let me conjure you by the rights of our fellowship, by the consonancy of our youth, by the obligation of our ever-preserved love, and by what more dear a better proposer could charge you withal, be even and direct with me, whether you were sent for or no.
>
> ROSECRANTZ. [*aside to Guildenstern*] What say you?
>
> HAMLET. [*aside*] Nay then, I have an eye of you.—If you love me, hold not off.
>
> GUILDENSTERN. My lord, we were sent for.
>
> HAMLET. I will tell you why. So shall my anticipation prevent your discovery, and your secrecy to the King and Queen moult no feather. I have of late—but wherefore I know not—lost all my mirth, forgone all custom of exercises; and indeed, it goes so heavily with my disposition that this goodly frame, the earth, seems to me a sterile promontory; this most excellent canopy, the air, look you, this brave o'erhanging firmament, this majestical roof fretted with golden fire—why, it appeareth no other thing to me than a foul and pestilent congregation of vapours. What a piece of work is a man! how noble in reason! how infinite in faculties! in form and moving how express and admirable! in action how like an angel! in apprehension how like a god! the beauty of the world, the paragon of animals! And yet to me what is this quintessence of dust? Man delights not me—no, nor woman neither, though by your smiling you seem to say so.
>
> ROSENCRANTZ. My lord, there was no such stuff in my thoughts.
>
> HAMLET. Why did you laugh then, when I said 'Man delights not me'?

> *Hamlet*, 2.2.296–321

In *Love's Labour's Lost*, Moth, the young servant to the pedant Don Armado, uses fantastical rhetoric while speaking in prose to make fun of his master:

> No, my complete master: but to jig off a tune at the tongue's end, canary to it with your feet, humour it with turning up your eyelids, sigh a **note** and sing a **note**, sometime through the **throat**, as if you swallowed love with singing love, sometime through the nose, as if you snuffed up love by smelling love; with your hat penthouse—like o'er the shop of your eyes; with your arms crossed on your thin-belly doublet like a rabbit on a spit; or your hands in your pocket like a man after the old painting; and keep not too long in one tune, but a snip and away. These are complements, these are humours; these betray nice wenches, that would be betrayed without these; and make them **men of note—do you note** me?—that most are affected to these.
>
> *Love's Labour's Lost*, 3.1.9–23

The point I want to make is that audiences are rarely aware whether an actor is speaking in verse or prose. The rhetorical devices that Shakespeare uses in verse, he also uses in prose, with the exception of regular meter. The stressed syllables still lift, however.

Rhyme in Prose

Sometimes you will find rhymes within Shakespeare's prose. In this example from *As You Like It*, Celia makes fun of a rather fussy courtier, Monsieur Le Beau, using rhyme, which sets up his entrance and gives the audience a sense of the character of the man.

> By my troth, thou sayest true; for since the little wit that fools have was silenced, the little foolery that wise men have makes a great **show**. Here comes Monsieur Le **Beau**.
>
> *As You Like It*, 1.2.72–74

Further Aspects of Shakespeare's Language

Actors will further enrich their performances of Shakespeare if they are aware of several other techniques or devices that he uses and how and why he does so. These other aspects of Shkespeare's language can range from the use of exposition and the sonnet form to the power of monosyllabic lines to the function of a narrator.

Monosyllabic Lines

Monosyllables have great emotional power as well as vocal effect. They can lift in pitch like a stressed syllable, but they are delivered slowly, and can be used in both verse and prose. The most famous line of monosyllabic lines may be Hamlet's "To be, or not to be—that is the question." It opens up a multitude of interpretive choices, as the slow monosyllables are open to a wide range of stresses leading to the double-stressed final word "question."

Early in the play, Hamlet mourns his father and the circumstances of his mother's marriage to his uncle in a series of monosyllables.

> That it should come to this!
> But two months dead! Nay, not so much, not two.
> *Hamlet* 1.2.137–52

When he waits for the bell that is the signal for Duncan's murder, Macbeth speaks in monosyllables, which slows the lines and increases the suspense:

> Whiles I threat he lives:
> Words to the heat of deeds too cold breath gives.
> I go, and it is done . . .
> *Macbeth*, 2.1.70–72

Long vowel sounds in one-syllable words are full of feeling. Note the use of assonance in the diphthong *oʊ*, which is always very emotional in Shakespeare.

- **Oh**, that I were a mockery king of snow
- Do not torment me! **Oh**!
- **Oh** pardon me in that my boast is true

but, O, methinks, how slow
This old moon wanes! she lingers my desires,
Like to a step-dame or a dowager
Long withering out a young man's revenue.
A Midsummer Night's Dream, 1.1.3–6

The diphthong aʊ is also deeply emotional in one-syllable words:
- Howl, Howl, Howl! O, you are men of stones!
- Down with him! Down with him!
- The law, for the which I think thou wilt howl

In the opening of *Richard III*, the assonance of the diphthong *aʊ*
in the monosyllables sets the mood for the rest of the play:

Now is the winter of **our** discontent
Made glorious summer by this son of York;
And all the cloud s that **lour'd** upon our **house**
In the deep bosom of the ocean buried.
Now are **our** b**rows** b**ound** with victorious wreaths;
Richard III, 1.1.1–5

In *Richard II*, when the king defies the nobles who have come to
depose him, he uses the diphthong *aʊ* to express his deep emotion:

But ere the cr**ow**n he looks for live in peace,
Ten th**ous**and bloody cr**ow**ns of mothers' sons
Shall ill become the fl**ow**er of England's face,
Richard II, 3.3.101–3

Exposition

Exposition gives information and explanation that is necessary to the
furtherance of the plot. It can be in prose or verse.

In act 1, scene 2, of *Macbeth*, a bleeding sergeant is brought
before King Duncan and, despite his wounds, describes in detail
the course of a battle in which Macbeth was valiant and proved victorious. After he is led off the battlefield, another character, Ross,
arrives, from whom we learn that the thane of Cawdor was a traitor
who assisted the Norwegian enemy but was defeated and captured.

The king then awards his title to Macbeth. This information is crucial to the working of the plot.

DUNCAN. What bloody man is that? He can report,
    As seemeth by his plight, of the revolt
    The newest state.
MALCOLM. This is the sergeant
    Who like a good and hardy soldier fought
    'Gainst my captivity. Hail, brave friend!
    Say to the king the knowledge of the broil
    As thou didst leave it.
SERGEANT. Doubtful it stood;
    As two spent swimmers, that do cling together
    And choke their art. The merciless Macdonwald—
    Worthy to be a rebel, for to that
    The multiplying villanies of nature
    Do swarm upon him—from the western isles
    Of kerns and gallowglasses is supplied;
    And fortune, on his damned quarrel smiling,
    Show'd like a rebel's whore: but all's too weak:
    For brave Macbeth—well he deserves that name—
    Disdaining fortune, with his brandish'd steel,
    Which smoked with bloody execution,
    Like valour's minion carved out his passage
    Till he faced the slave;
    Which ne'er shook hands, nor bade farewell to him,
    Till he unseam'd him from the nave to the chaps,
    And fix'd his head upon our battlements.
DUNCAN. O valiant cousin! worthy gentleman!
. . . .
SERGEANT. But I am faint, my gashes cry for help.
DUNCAN. So well thy words become thee as thy wounds;
    They smack of honour both. Go get him surgeons.
    Who comes here?
MALCOLM. The worthy thane of Ross.
. . . .

ROSS. God save the king!

DUNCAN. Whence camest thou, worthy thane?

ROSS. From Fife, great king;
>   Where the Norweyan banners flout the sky
>   And fan our people cold. Norway himself,
>   With terrible numbers,
>   Assisted by that most disloyal traitor
>   The thane of Cawdor, began a dismal conflict;
>   Till that Bellona's bridegroom, lapp'd in proof,
>   Confronted him with self-comparisons,
>   Point against point rebellious, arm 'gainst arm.
>   Curbing his lavish spirit: and, to conclude,
>   The victory fell on us.

. . . .

DUNCAN. No more that thane of Cawdor shall deceive
>   Our bosom interest: go pronounce his present death,
>   And with his former title greet Macbeth.

ROSS. I'll see it done.

DUNCAN. What he hath lost noble Macbeth hath won.

Macbeth, 1.2.1–26, 46–50, 53–65, 72–76

Enjambment

An enjambed line is a line whose sense continues as it is carried to the next line. The inflection may lift at the end of the line, giving it forward momentum as the thought caries through to the next line, but it is not necessary to take a breath.

>   What if this cursèd hand
> Were thicker than itself with brother's blood,
> Is there not rain enough in the sweet heavens
> To wash it white as snow?

Hamlet, 3.3.48–51

Notice that the lines are a rhetorical question.

End-Stopping

An end-stopped line in verse ends with a mark of punctuation such as a comma, a semicolon, or a colon. The syntax is contained in that one line, and the actor can take a quick breath on an upward inflection before the next line.

> Now climbeth Tamora Olympus' top,
> Safe out of fortune's shot; and sits aloft,
> Secure of thunder's crack or lightning flash;
> Advanced above pale envy's threatening reach.
>
> *Titus Andronicus*, 2.1.1–4

Caesura

A caesura is a pause in a line of verse that is formed by the rhythms of natural speech and may occur near the middle or toward the end of a line of verse. It is not usually marked with punctuation, although some editions may have added a comma. This gives the actor a choice as to where or whether to take the pause. The caesura pause is very quick—don't breathe on it.

> There may be in the cup
> A spider steep'd, and one may drink, depart,
> And yet partake no venom, for his knowledge
> Is not infected: but if one present
> The abhorr'd ingredient to his eye, make known
> What he hath drunk, he cracks his gorge, his sides,
> With violent hefts. I have drunk, and seen the spider.
>
> *The Winter's Tale*, 2.1.50–56

The Sonnet

Sonnets were the rage in Shakespeare's time. Originally introduced by Sir Thomas Wyatt (who narrowly escaped execution by Henry VIII) and the Earl of Surrey (who did not escape), English sonnets were strongly influenced by the Italian sonnets of Petrarch. Shakespeare's sonnets are the products of an oral culture. An educated person at the court of Queen Elizabeth I would have been expected to speak extemporaneously in blank verse and to be well versed in all the forms of rhetoric.

Shakespeare's sonnets were published separately and, as far as we know, without his permission.

The two types of sonnets—Petrarchian/Italian and Shakespearian/Elizabethan—differ in their arrangement of the rhyme scheme. The Italian sonnet is older and consists of an octave and a sestet with the rhyme scheme being *abbaabba* in the octave and *cdecde* or some other variation in the sestet. The English rhyme scheme consists of three quatrains and a couplet with the rhyme scheme being as follows: *abab cdcd efef gg*.

A sonnet explores an idea, a thought, or a feeling within fourteen highly structured lines of iambic pentameter and finally sums up or resolves the theme introduced at the beginning in the final lines, usually in the sestet or the couplet.

> So are you to my thoughts as food to life,
> Or as sweet-season'd showers are to the ground;
> And for the peace of you I hold such strife
> As 'twixt a miser and his wealth is found;
> Now proud as an enjoyer and anon
> Doubting the filching age will steal his treasure,
> Now counting best to be with you alone,
> Then better'd that the world may see my pleasure;
> Sometime all full with feasting on your sight
> And by and by clean starved for a look;
> Possessing or pursuing no delight,
> Save what is had or must from you be took.
> Thus do I pine and surfeit day by day,
> Or gluttoning on all, or all away.
>
> Sonnet 75.1–14

Speaking the Sonnet

Speaking verse requires intense focus as well as energy. What is the theme, the argument, the point to be made? A sonnet has a theme that is usually introduced in the first two or three lines, explored, then resolved or concluded toward the end of the sonnet or in the couplet.

So are you to my thoughts as food to life, (breath)
Or as sweet-season'd showers are to the ground (breath)

Sonnet 75.1–2

Take a catch breath at the end of each line, but connect the sense to the following line. The breath fuels the thought and enables the audience to follow the exposition of the theme.

And for the peace of you I hold such strife (breath)
As 'twixt a miser and his wealth is found; (breath)

Sonnet 75.3–4

Intone lines of a sonnet—feel the sense in the resonance of the words. Get a sense of the sounds on your tongue and lips.

Note the use of antithesis, as in "miser and his wealth" or "pine and surfeit." And be aware of the alliteration, assonance, and word-play in the lines, as in "sweet-season'd showers" (alliteration) and "**Dou**bting the filching age will steal his treasure, / Now **cou**nting best to be with you alone" (assonance).

Don't let the last word in each line drop. In iambic pentameter the last word in the line is stressed: "Thus do I pine and surfeit day by dáy, / Or gluttoning on all, or all awáy."

Sonnets are important for actors because they explore all the structural rules of classical texts. Every actor should have at least one or two sonnets memorized—they are sometimes asked for in an audition.

Sonnets in Shakespeare's Plays

The sonnet structure is also found in Shakespeare's plays in a variety of forms.

In *Romeo and Juliet* alone, the sonnet structure appears several times. The prologue gives a synopsis of the play and is written as a sonnet. It could played by one actor or by several, spoken by the townspeople of Verona.

Two households, both alike in dignity,
In fair Verona, where we lay our scene,
From ancient grudge break to new mutiny,
Where civil blood makes civil hands unclean.

From forth the fatal loins of these two foes
A pair of star-cross'd lovers take their life;
Whose misadventured piteous overthrows
Do with their death bury their parents' strife.
The fearful passage of their death-mark'd love,
And the continuance of their parents' rage,
Which, but their children's end, nought could remove,
Is now the two hours' traffic of our stage;
The which if you with patient ears attend,
What here shall miss, our toil shall strive to mend.

Romeo and Juliet, prologue.1–14

Romeo and Juliet meet at a ball at the Capulets' house. Their dialogue, spoken in shared lines as they dance, takes the form of a sonnet:

ROMEO. If I profane with my unworthiest hand
    This holy shrine, the gentle fine is this:
    My lips, two blushing pilgrims, ready stand
    To smooth that rough touch with a tender kiss.
JULIET. Good pilgrim, you do wrong your hand too much,
    Which mannerly devotion shows in this;
    For saints have hands that pilgrims' hands do touch,
    And palm to palm is holy palmers' kiss.
ROMEO. Have not saints lips, and holy palmers too?
JULIET. Ay, pilgrim, lips that they must use in prayer.
ROMEO. O, then, dear saint, let lips do what hands do;
    They pray, grant thou, lest faith turn to despair.
JULIET. Saints do not move, though grant for prayers' sake.
ROMEO. Then move not, while my prayer's effect I take.
    Thus from my lips, by yours, my sin is purged.
JULIET. Then have my lips the sin that they have took.
ROMEO. Sin from thy lips? O trespass sweetly urged!
    Give me my sin again.
JULIET. You kiss by the book.

Romeo and Juliet, 1.5.100–118

A third example of the sonnet form used as plot device comes at the beginning of Act 2 just before the balcony scene. The character, simply called "Chorus," calls the audience's attention to the end of Romeo's infatuation with Rosaline and to his new love of Juliet:

> Now old desire doth in his death-bed lie,
> And young affection gapes to be his heir;
> That fair for which love groan'd for and would die,
> With tender Juliet match'd, is now not fair.
> Now Romeo is beloved and loves again,
> Alike betwitched by the charm of looks,
> But to his foe supposed he must complain,
> And she steal love's sweet bait from fearful hooks:
> Being held a foe, he may not have access
> To breathe such vows as lovers use to swear;
> And she as much in love, her means much less
> To meet her new-beloved any where:
> But passion lends them power, time means, to meet
> Tempering extremities with extreme sweet.
>
> *Romeo and Juliet*, 2.prologue.1–14

Telling the Story

In part because Shakespeare's theater used little or no scenery, he relied on the spoken word to set the scene. He would sometimes create a character to act as the narrator of the scene. The following practice selections provide examples of the ways Shakespeare used verse and prose with his narrators to provide and explain background information and story twists.

Practice Selection: *Henry V* **Prologue**

In the following speech from *Henry V*, a character referred to in the script as simply "Chorus" describes the atmosphere in the English camp the night before the battle of Agincourt, which sets the stage for what is to follow. Let's now explore the rhetorical devices that Shakespeare used to create that atmosphere.

The first thing to ask is: Is it in verse or prose? I think just the pattern on the page tells us that it is in verse. Is it regular iambic or is the first beat on the first syllable? Let's go through the text and see how we can apply some of the principles we have explored in the earlier chapters to speaking the text.

Now entertain conjecture of a time
When creeping murmur and the poring dark
Fills the wide vessel of the universe.
From camp to camp through the foul womb of night
The hum of either army stilly sounds,
That the fixed sentinels almost receive
The secret whispers of each other's watch:
Fire answers fire, and through their paly flames
Each battle sees the other's umber'd face;
Steed threatens steed, in high and boastful neighs
Piercing the night's dull ear, and from the tents
The armourers, accomplishing the knights,
With busy hammers closing rivets up,
Give dreadful note of preparation:
The country cocks do crow, the clocks do toll,
And the third hour of drowsy morning name.
Proud of their numbers and secure in soul,
The confident and over-lusty French
Do the low-rated English play at dice;
And chide the cripple tardy-gaited night
Who, like a foul and ugly witch, doth limp
So tediously away. The poor condemned English,
Like sacrifices, by their watchful fires
Sit patiently and inly ruminate
The morning's danger, and their gesture sad
Investing lank-lean; cheeks and war-worn coats
Presenteth them unto the gazing moon
So many horrid ghosts. O now, who will behold
The royal captain of this ruin'd band
Walking from watch to watch, from tent to tent,
Let him cry 'Praise and glory on his head!'
For forth he goes and visits all his host.

Bids them good morrow with a modest smile
And calls them brothers, friends and countrymen.
Upon his royal face there is no note
How dread an army hath enrounded him;
Nor doth he dedicate one jot of colour
Unto the weary and all-watched night,
But freshly looks and over-bears attaint
With cheerful semblance and sweet majesty;
That every wretch, pining and pale before,
Beholding him, plucks comfort from his looks:
A largess universal like the sun
His liberal eye doth give to every one,
Thawing cold fear, that mean and gentle all,
Behold, as may unworthiness define,
A little touch of Harry in the night.
And so our scene must to the battle fly;
Where—O for pity!—we shall much disgrace
With four or five most vile and ragged foils,
Right ill-disposed in brawl ridiculous,
The name of Agincourt. Yet sit and see,
Minding true things by what their mockeries be.

Henry V, 4.prologue.1–52

Practice Selection: *Pericles, Prince of Tyre* Prologue

In *Pericles, Prince of Tyre*, the character of Gower, a legendary
early medieval poet, is the narrator who appears throughout the
play to help the audience understand the rather complicated story.
Notice that the character speaks in rhymed tetrameter with four
beats to the line and not iambic pentameter. Don't let the lines
become sing-song; focus on the operative words, making your
points as you lift the pitch on the stressed syllables. One line of
the speech is in Latin: *Et bonum quo antiquius, eo melius*, which
translates as "the older, the better."

To sing a song that old was sung,
From ashes ancient Gower is come;
Assuming man's infirmities,
To glad your ear, and please your eyes.
It hath been sung at festivals,
On ember-eves and holy-ales;
And lords and ladies in their lives
Have read it for restoratives:
The purchase is to make men glorious;
Et bonum quo antiquius, eo melius.
If you, born in these latter times,
When wit's more ripe, accept my rhymes.
And that to hear an old man sing
May to your wishes pleasure bring
I life would wish, and that I might
Waste it for you, like taper-light.
This Antioch, then, Antiochus the Great
Built up, this city, for his chiefest seat:
The fairest in all Syria,
I tell you what mine authors say:
This king unto him took a fere,
Who died and left a female heir,
So buxom, blithe, and full of face,
As heaven had lent her all his grace;
With whom the father liking took,
And her to incest did provoke:
Bad child; worse father! to entice his own
To evil should be done by none:
But custom what they did begin
Was with long use account no sin.
The beauty of this sinful dame
Made many princes thither frame,
To seek her as a bed-fellow,
In marriage-pleasures play-fellow:
Which to prevent he made a law,
To keep her still, and men in awe,
That whoso ask'd her for his wife,
His riddle told not, lost his life:
So for her many a wight did die,

As yon grim looks do testify.
What now ensues, to the judgment of your eye
I give, my cause who best can justify.

Pericles, Prince of Tyre, 1.prologue.1–42

Practice Selection: *Troilus and Cressida* Prologue

In *Troilus and Cressida*, the prologue begins the play, giving the background story of the Trojan War and letting the audience know that the play begins in the middle of the war, but that it doesn't necessarily finish with the end of the war. This prologue is in iambic pentameter and ends in four lines of rhymed couplets.

In Troy, there lies the scene. From isles of Greece
The princes orgulous, their high blood chafed,
Have to the port of Athens sent their ships,
Fraught with the ministers and instruments
Of cruel war: sixty and nine, that wore
Their crownets regal, from the Athenian bay
Put forth toward Phrygia; and their vow is made
To ransack Troy, within whose strong immures
The ravish'd Helen, Menelaus' queen,
With wanton Paris sleeps; and that's the quarrel.
To Tenedos they come;
And the deep-drawing barks do there disgorge
Their warlike fraughtage: now on Dardan plains
The fresh and yet unbruised Greeks do pitch
Their brave pavilions: Priam's six-gated city,
Dardan, and Tymbria, Helias, Chetas, Troien,
And Antenorides, with massy staples
And corresponsive and fulfilling bolts,
Sperr up the sons of Troy.
Now expectation, tickling skittish spirits,
On one and other side, Trojan and Greek,
Sets all on hazard: and hither am I come
A prologue arm'd, but not in confidence
Of author's pen or actor's voice, but suited

In like conditions as our argument,
To tell you, fair beholders, that our play
Leaps o'er the vaunt and firstlings of those broils,
Beginning in the middle, starting thence away
To what may be digested in a play.
Like or find fault; do as your pleasures are:
Now good or bad, 'tis but the chance of war.

Troilus and Cressida, I.prologue.1–31

Practice Selection: *Antony and Cleopatra*

In *Antony and Cleopatra*, Enobarbus, a Roman soldier and Antony's friend, describes Cleopatra's first meeting with Antony to two of his friends. The speech begins in prose, and quickly moves to verse:

When she first met Mark Antony, she pursed up his heart, upon the river of Cydnus.

. . . .

The barge she sat in, like a burnish'd throne,
Burn'd on the water: the poop was beaten gold;
Purple the sails, and so perfumed that
The winds were love-sick with them; the oars were silver,
Which to the tune of flutes kept stroke, and made
The water which they beat to follow faster,
As amorous of their strokes. For her own person,
It beggar'd all description: she did lie
In her pavilion—cloth-of-gold of tissue—
O'er-picturing that Venus where we see
The fancy outwork nature: on each side her
Stood pretty dimpled boys, like smiling Cupids,
With divers-colour'd fans, whose wind did seem
To glow the delicate cheeks which they did cool,
And what they undid did.

. . . .

Her gentlewomen, like the Nereides,
So many mermaids, tended her i' the eyes,

And made their bends adornings: at the helm
A seeming mermaid steers: the silken tackle
Swell with the touches of those flower-soft hands,
That yarely frame the office. From the barge
A strange invisible perfume hits the sense
Of the adjacent wharfs. The city cast
Her people out upon her; and Antony,
Enthroned i' the market-place, did sit alone,
Whistling to the air; which, but for vacancy,
Had gone to gaze on Cleopatra too,
And made a gap in nature.

. . . .

Upon her landing, Antony sent to her,
Invited her to supper: she replied,
It should be better he became her guest;
Which she entreated: our courteous Antony,
Whom ne'er the word of 'No' woman heard speak,
Being barber'd ten times o'er, goes to the feast,
And for his ordinary pays his heart
For what his eyes eat only.

. . . .

Age cannot wither her, nor custom stale
Her infinite variety: other women cloy
The appetites they feed: but she makes hungry
Where most she satisfies . . .

Antony and Cleopatra, 2.2.229–30, 234–48,
250–62, 264–71, 282–85

Practice Selection: *The Winter's Tale*

In *The Winter's Tale*, sixteen years separate the first half of
the play from the second half, which introduces a host of new
characters, as well as some of the characters from the first act.
Shakespeare uses the device of Time, a character who functions
as a prologue to the play and brings the audience up to date with
what has transpired before the second half of the play begins.

Time's speech is in blank verse (iambic pentameter), using rhymed couplets.

I, that please some, try all, both joy and terror
Of good and bad, that makes and unfolds error,
Now take upon me, in the name of Time,
To use my wings. Impute it not a crime
To me or my swift passage, that I slide
O'er sixteen years and leave the growth untried
Of that wide gap, since it is in my power
To o'erthrow law and in one self-born hour
To plant and o'erwhelm custom. Let me pass
The same I am, ere ancient'st order was
Or what is now received: I witness to
The times that brought them in; so shall I do
To the freshest things now reigning and make stale
The glistering of this present, as my tale
Now seems to it. Your patience this allowing,
I turn my glass and give my scene such growing
As you had slept between: Leontes leaving,
The effects of his fond jealousies so grieving
That he shuts up himself, imagine me,
Gentle spectators, that I now may be
In fair Bohemia, and remember well,
I mentioned a son o' the king's, which Florizel
I now name to you; and with speed so pace
To speak of Perdita, now grown in grace
Equal with wondering: what of her ensues
I list not prophecy; but let Time's news
Be known when 'tis brought forth.
A shepherd's daughter,
And what to her adheres, which follows after,
Is the argument of Time. Of this allow,
If ever you have spent time worse ere now;
If never, yet that Time himself doth say
He wishes earnestly you never may.

The Winter's Tale, 4.1.1–32

A Final Note

In all this discussion of verse and prose, we need to remember that Shakespeare's language served the needs of a theater that performed in daylight; had little or no scenery, lights, period costumes, or special effects; and relied on the words spoken by the actors to hold the audience's attention. This is what still draws audiences to Shakespeare's plays, and when the language becomes secondary to the stage effects, the audience loses.

6

Which Text Is Shakespeare's Text?

We have the text to guide us, half a dozen stage directions and that is all. I abide by the text and the demands of the text and beyond that I claim freedom.

—Harley Granville-Barker

Harley Granville-Barker (1877–1946) was a British actor, director, playwright, critic, and theorist who is credited with being one of the first directors to insist that Shakespeare's text was the foundation for his productions, eschewing the elaborate sets, lighting, and production details that the nineteenth-century British theater had relied on. In Granville-Barker's productions of Shakespeare, he favored natural speech rhythms performed on a bare stage, with scenes that moved quickly from one to another. After retiring from the stage in the early 1920s, Granville-Barker wrote his *Prefaces to Shakespeare*, which examine the text of ten of Shakespeare's plays in great detail and are still considered among the most important sources for understanding Shakespeare's plays today.[1]

But what text is Granville-Barker talking about when he says, "I abide by the text and the demands of the text"? There are a great many contemporary editions of Shakespeare that I have consulted in writing this book: the Arden, the Oxford, the Cambridge, the RSC, the Pelican, the Riverside, the Norton, the Yale, and the New Folger Library, as well as the First Folio—and that's only a small sample.

There are also a great many online editions. Given all these choices, what is an actor or director to do when selecting a printed copy of Shakespeare's plays to perform or direct?

My experience as a vocal coach and director for a good number of Shakespeare theaters is that the director usually selects a text for the acting company based on the reputation of the editor of the text, the size of the script (which facilitates the ease of holding it during rehearsals), and most importantly—the price. Shakespeare's plays require a large cast. To supplement the acting script, there are copies of other editions, including the First Folio, on the rehearsal table for the actors and director to consult.

Sometimes an actor will come across a line that ends in a semicolon in one edition, a comma in another, a colon in another, or even a period or full stop. I asked several Shakespeare theaters how they arrived at a script. Alan Paul, a former student of mine at Northwestern University and now the associate artistic director of the Shakespeare Theatre Company in Washington, D.C., consulted with the theater's dramaturg, Drew Licthenberg:

> We use the Arden (sometimes both the Arden 2 from the '60s–'70s and the more modern Arden 3 editions), the Oxford (c. 1990s), and the New Cambridge (c. 1980s). These will then lead me back to textual choices from the Folio and Quarto editions, but it takes some close reading of different editors and their biases. It's more to me about reading widely and then selectively undoing/redoing some of the editorial work if that makes sense. Michael Khan (the artistic director) usually works from the Arden and a lifetime of practice in the room.[2]

At the Chicago Shakespeare Theater, when I was the vocal coach for *Love's Labour's Lost*, the theater used the First Folio as its chief guide, with the text typed directly from the Folio for ease in reading, but words could still be changed by the director for clarity. In reply to an email I sent, Barbara Gaines, the artistic director of Chicago Shakespeare, who also directed *Love's Labour's Lost*, said:

> For plays that I direct we use the First Folio, with additional help from the Quartos, if necessary. Other directors choose what editions suit them best. In the Folio, the punctuation,

capitalizations, and the way the verse is set upon the page can be of great use to directors and actors. The Folio technique is a guide that can help unlock Shakespeare's texts—they're all theatrical tools for us to use or ignore. And yes, we type the Folio scripts.[3]

It is very surprising how different all the editions are, not just in terms of punctuation but in word use. Why is this? Why should there be so many variations in Shakespeare's text? The answer is that during Shakespeare's lifetime there was not just one definitive text, but many. Here is a rough explanation.

The Quartos

Shakespeare's plays began to be printed in 1594, probably with his tragedy *Titus Andronicus*. This appeared as a small, cheap pamphlet called a quarto because of the way it was printed—a sheet of paper folded in half and then folded again to make four sides. Eighteen of Shakespeare's plays had appeared in quarto editions by the time of his death in 1616. Another three plays were printed in quarto before 1642. Since the plays were not protected by copyright but were the property of the theater that paid for them, there were only one or two copies of the play available, and they were closely guarded. The actors were given cue sheets with only their own lines written on them, along with cue words indicating the words spoken by the actor whose line came before his and was the cue for him to speak.

Why Are the Quartos Important?

None of Shakespeare's manuscripts survived, so the printed texts of his plays are our only source for what he originally wrote. The quarto editions are the texts closest to Shakespeare's time. Some are thought to preserve either his working drafts (foul papers) or his fair copies. Others are thought to record versions remembered by the actors who performed the plays, or prompt books providing information about staging practices in Shakespeare's day. There are bad quartos, probably stolen or surreptitiously copied during a performance, and good quartos, which for some reason were sold by the company, but regardless, they are important sources for Shakespearean scholars studying his works. There are, for example, two quartos of *Hamlet*. Q1 (Quarto 1) was published in 1603 and attributed to William Shakespeare, claiming that it was "diverse times acted by his Highnesse seruants in the Cittie of London: as also in the two Vniuersities of Cambridge and Oxford, and elsewhere." In 1604 another quarto, Q2, was published, which claimed to be "Newly imprinted and enlarged to almost as much againe as it was, according to the true and perfect Coppie." Q1 is considered a "bad" quarto, and Q2 the "good" quarto."[4]

The First Folio

In 1623, seven years after Shakespeare's death, an expensive volume of thirty-six of his plays was published by John Heminges and Henry Condell, actors and shareholders in Shakespeare's company. This was the First Folio, which included most of the plays printed in quarto form and introduced eighteen plays that had never been printed before. These included *All's Well That Ends Well, Antony and Cleopatra, As You Like it, The Comedy of Errors, Coriolanus, Cymbeline, Henry VI, Part 1, Part 2,* and *Part 3, Henry VIII, Julius Caesar, King John, Macbeth, Measure for Measure, The Taming of the Shrew, The Tempest, Timon of Athens, Twelfth Night, Two Gentlemen of Verona,* and *The Winter's Tale. Pericles* was not included in the First Folio and only appeared in later editions. The edition was compiled from Shakespeare's "foul papers" or unedited manuscripts, prompt books, and perhaps sides or cue scripts from members of his company. It was meant to bring together all of his plays that had been published as quartos and also to correct "stol'n and surreptitious copies, maimed and deformed by frauds and stealths of injurious impostors." The editors declared that the Folio contained Shakespeare's true words and "are now offer'd to your view cured, and perfect of their limbes; and all the rest, absolute in their numbers as he conceived them."[5]

Shakespeare's Punctuation in the First Folio

English punctuation has changed radically in the last four hundred years. Modern punctuation is, or at any rate attempts to be, *grammatical* for ease in reading; the earlier system was mainly *rhetorical* to facilitate oral communication. Some directors use the original Folio believing that it is the closest to Shakespeare's original text, especially with regard to punctuation. Of course, since none of Shakespeare's original manuscripts survived, we have no way of knowing whether the punctuation in the First Folio was really Shakespeare's punctuation or one of the several printers who worked on it.

One result of a rhetorical versus a grammatical system of punctuation is the use of fewer periods, or full stops. According to George Puttenham's *The Art of English Poesie 1589*, "the shortest pause or intermission they call the 'comma' as who would say a piece of speech cut off."[6] There was a wider use of the comma then as compared to today's use of the semicolon and colon. We base our punctuation now on structure and grammatical form; the old system was largely guided by an attempt to convey the meaning phonetically.[7]

Look at the *rhetorical* punctuation of this short excerpt from *Twelth Night*:

> Too old by heaven: Let still the woman take
> An elder than herself, so wears she to him;
> So sways she level in her husband's heart;
> *Twelfth Night* (First Folio), 2.4.33–35[8]

Here is the same short excerpt with *grammatical* punctuation:

> Too old, by heaven. Let still the woman take
> An elder than herself. So wears she to him;
> So sways she level in her husband's heart.
> *Twelfth Night* (The New Folger Library), 2.4.34–36[9]

The meaning is subtly changed by the modern punctuation because a period or full stop encourages the inflection of the voice to drop down as if the thought is ending, rather than inflect up for a continuing thought.

Capitalization and the First Folio

According to David Crystal, the noted British linguist and editor of *The Cambridge Encyclopedia of the English Language*, it seems to have been a common practice in Britain in the seventeenth and eighteenth centuries to capitalize the first letter of nouns.[10] This practice was even used by Benjamin Franklin in his *Autobiography*. Franklin worked for several years as a printer's apprentice in England and may have picked up the practice there:

> My Mother, the second wife of Abiah Folger, a Daughter of Peter Folger, one of the Settlers of New England, of whom honorable mention was made by Cotton Mather, in his Church History of that Country, entitled Magnalia Christi Americana) as a *godly learned Englishman,* if I remember the words rightly.[11]

I'm not sure we can say that the capitalization that is found in the printed Folio is something that Shakespeare intended to be an indication of meaning. We have no surviving manuscript of his plays, and as the Folio was published after Shakespeare's death, we simply don't know.

The First Folio and Performance

Recently some theater companies and directors have begun working exclusively with the First Folio, believing that it is the closest one can get to the original text of Shakespeare as performed by his company and that it gives performance clues to actors through capitalization, punctuation, and some changes or omissions of words. Chicago Shakespeare Theater uses the First Folio as a guide, although visiting directors are free to make different choices.[12]

Shakespeare after the Folio

When I was an acting student in the drama department at Carnegie Tech (now Carnegie Mellon), I was given a monologue of Katherine's from *The Taming of the Shrew* by one of my teachers in acting class. I liked the monologue, memorized it, and performed it in class. A few years later, in my first professional production at the San Francisco Actor's Workshop, I was performing the role of Bianca, Katherine's younger sister in *The Taming of the Shrew*. I remember reading the play and being very puzzled because I couldn't find Katherine's monologue, the one I had memorized in acting class—it just wasn't in the play. I could still remember the lines, but the monologue had vanished. When I mentioned this to the director, Robert Symonds, he looked at me a bit strangely and told me that he had never heard of it. As I was researching this chapter, I suddenly remembered that monologue. I searched for it online, and there it was:

> KATHERINE. Why, yes; sister Bianca now shall see,
> The poor abandoned Katharine, as she calls me,
> Can make her husband stoop unto her lure.
> And hold her head as high, and be as proud.
> As she, or e'er a wife in Padua.
> As double as my portion be my scorn!
> Look to your seat, Petruchio, or I throw you:
> Katharine shall tame this haggard; or, if she fails,
> Shall tie her tongue up, and pare down her nails.[13]

I still like the monologue, but it is not Shakespeare: it's from David Garrick, one of the eighteenth century's greatest actors, who was also producer, playwright, and manager of the Drury Lane Theatre in London.

Shakespeare and the English Revolution

In 1642, only thirty-nine years after the death of Queen Elizabeth I and after a series of conflicts, civil war broke out in England. The two sides consisted of the Royalists and the Puritans, who both held strong views when it came to the theater. The Royalists strongly supported the theater, while the Puritans considered theaters dens of vice and demanded that they be banned. The Puritans won the war, with the result that King Charles I lost his head, and the theaters were closed. The Puritans went even further, prohibiting the performance of plays and outlawing actors as rogues and vagabonds. The king's son, Charles, fled to France, where he lived in exile at the French court of Louis XIV. In London, theaters fell into disrepair or were torn down, and actors had to fend for themselves.

Shakespeare and the Restoration

With the restoration of the monarchy in 1660, the theaters reopened and the new king, Charles II, awarded a monopoly for theatrical production to two of his favorite courtiers, Sir Thomas Killigrew and Sir William Davenant. Because the Puritans didn't object to music, Sir William had produced several operas during the *interregnum,* and his tastes were in line with those of the new king's, which had been cultivated along the classic lines preferred by the French. It fell to Sir William Davenant to produce plays of Shakespeare.

It was to be a very different kind of Shakespeare for a very different kind of audience. Instead of the large audiences of different classes who flocked to the Globe, the audience in this period consisted mainly of aristocrats and the well-to-do. Also, the new theaters were much smaller, as were the audiences. Under Sir William Davenant almost all of Shakespeare's plays were "improved."

According to Barbara A. Murray,

> The newly-formed King's Company (Killigrew) and Duke's Company (Davenant) had no option but to rely on the pre–Civil War repertory, most particularly the printed folio works of Shakespeare, Jonson, and Beaumont and Fletcher. Of these three sources, Shakespeare was the least valued because his plays were most at odds with prevailing literary and theatrical tastes. It is a sign of Shakespeare's perceived demerits that Charles's favorite, Killigrew, was awarded rights to the more desirable plays of Jonson and Fletcher, supplemented by a small portion of Shakespeare's texts. Davenant, by contrast, had to make do with his own plays and the remainder of Shakespeare's corpus. With only a handful of exceptions, Shakespeare's plays were vigorously rewritten for performance on the Restoration stage.[14]

Davenant rewrote *Macbeth, a Tragedy*, with "all the alterations, amendments, additions and new songs," in 1674. He gave lots of music and dancing to the witches, cut the Porter, and expanded the role of Lady Macduff, balancing the virtuous Macduffs with the evil, murderous Macbeths. Davenant's version of *Macbeth* replaced Shakespeare's for eighty years.

In an adaptation of *King Lear* by Nahum Tate, the Fool was cut, King Lear was restored to his throne, and Cordelia and Edgar were made into heroic lovers who were reunited at the end of the play, swearing vengeance on Gonerill and Regan.

My absolute favorite is a version of *Henry V,* adapted by Aaron Hill, which introduces Harriet, a young love interest for the king, who then betrays her so he can marry a French princess. Here is an example of her outraged monologue:

> HARRIET. Reason?—I deteste it—
>   'Tis that, which gives an Edge to all my Sufferings!
>   Am I not lost, disgrac'd, forsaken, scorn'd?
>   And owe I not this Ruin to my Love?
>   Has not the Man, I doted on, destroy'd me?
>   He, for whose sake I had no Ear for Honour!
>   Has he not left me, like a common Creature,
>   And *paid* me, like a Prostitute—Death find Him!
>   Has he not offer'd me a fancy Pension.
>   Told out the Hire of Infamy? and judg'd
>   Wealth an Equivalent for my Undoing?
>   Has he not dar'd all This?—and does He now,
>   While my Disgrace is new, freshblown, and flagrant,
>   Now, does he think to live, and wed another!
>   Calm? No—Let Cottage Fools, with helpless Sighs,
>   Bewail their ruin'd Innocence—My Soul,
>   Full charg'd with Hate, and Pride, breaks out in Passion,
>   Bold, as my Wrongs, and dreadfull, as my Purpose.
>   *Henry V*, Aaron Hill's 1723 adaptation[15]

I have copied the exact punctuation of the printed text, and it is interesting that the capitalization of nouns still follows the style of the First Folio. Since Shakespeare had no say in the style of printing of that eighteenth-century script, perhaps those directors who are relying on the capitalizations in the First Folio as guides to performance should rethink being quite so adamant.

Eighteenth-Century Attempts at Restoration of Shakespeare's Text

In the eighteenth century, there was a movement to restore Shakespeare to his original text, led by none other than David Garrick, the author of my monologue from *The Taming of the Shrew*. I found the play online in a prompt book of Edwin Booth's that listed it as the *Romantic Comedy of Katharine and Petruchio*. There is an introduction, which says:

> The stage copy of "The Taming of the Shrew," which, under the name of *Katharine and Petruchio*, has for many years been in common use, was made by Garrick. The present version—giving the text and the stage-business used by Edwin Booth—is an alteration of that piece. The original play, which, obviously, is much better in the reading than it would be in the representation, is never acted. (October 15, 1878)[16]

It is clear that when Abraham Lincoln complained that the productions of Shakespeare that he saw in the theaters in Washington, D.C., were different from the printed texts that he read on his own, he was right—they were different. Edwin Booth used David Garrick's eighteenth-century adaptations of Shakespeare in his own productions in America. Booth also declares that the "original play, much better, is never acted." According to Frances E. Dolan, between 1754 and 1844, *Catharine and Petruchio* was the only version of Shakespeare's play performed on British and American stages, and the sixth most popular Shakespearean play. It was so popular that Katherine's monologue was still being used in acting classes well into the twentieth century.

Of course, there were copies of Shakespeare's plays printed after the Restoration that weren't rewritten, but only *Henry VIII* seems to have been performed in Shakespeare's original text.[17]

New Editions of Shakespeare in Eighteenth-Century London

The London theater in the eighteenth century was a lively and popular enterprise. Shakespeare became one of the most popular playwrights, and his plays were widely performed, although, as we have seen, not in their original form.

Publishing at this time was still mostly in the hands of booksellers who also served as publishers, and anyone could publish almost anything as long as they could pay for it. As far as publishing Shakespeare's text, many did.

In 1709, Nicholas Rowe, playwright, dramatist, and soon-to-be poet laureate, was one of the first editors to regularize Shakespeare's text, using the Fourth Folio and adding lists of characters and stage directions. The poet Alexander Pope, famous for his heroic couplets and his satiric *The Rape of the Lock*, managed to support himself on subscriptions of his edited Shakespeare, much of which he is reported to have lifted from Rowe's editions. There were nine or ten editions of Shakespeare edited by other writers, mostly copying from Rowe, the Fourth Folio, and one another.

One of the most interesting editions was by Samuel Johnson, English literary critic, biographer, poet, playwright, and one of the most towering literary figures of the eighteenth century. Johnson is especially famous for his *Dictionary of the English Language*, which he wrote singlehandedly, and which had a profound effect on the English language. Always short of money, in 1756 Johnson published his *Proposals for Printing, by Subscription, the Dramatick Works of William Shakespeare*, which he said had been so poorly edited that he needed to "correct what is corrupt, and to explain what is obscure." He took so long to finish (nine years) that a poet named Charles Churchill wrote teasingly: "He for subscribers baits his hook / And takes your cash, but where's the book?"[18] Johnson was originally the schoolmaster and then a friend of Garrick.

To support the number of these prestigious publications, the copyright to Shakespeare's works was owned by a bookseller, Jacob Tonson, who published the Shakespeare editions of Nicholas Rowe and Alexander Pope as well as other expensive books. In 1709 a Copyright Act was passed that stated that "any 'rights' that the firm previously held would expire in 1731."[19] At first Tonson ignored this new law, but other booksellers began to sell cheaper copies, with the result that the market was flooded with inexpensive copies of Shakespeare's plays, bringing the Bard into contact with a huge audience of ordinary readers for the first time.

In the early nineteenth century, several variorum editions of Shakespeare's collected works were published. These editions attempted to collate the different editions, including one by James Boswell, friend and biographer of Samuel Johnson. All these editions were compiled by gentlemen of letters and means who were not professional scholars or connected to any academic institution.

The Cambridge Edition of Wright and Clark

In 1864, William George Clark and William Aldis Wright set out to publish an edited version of Shakespeare's plays, drawing on two or more texts. They were both fellows at Trinity College, Cambridge, and literary and classical scholars. The Cambridge edition was published in nine volumes between 1863 and 1893, with the text based on the four Folios and all the Quarto editions and with the base text being the 1623 Folio. It was a work of enormous scholarship intended for a well-to-do class of readers who could afford the £9 ($100 today) for the set.

The Globe Edition of Shakespeare

In 1864, a Scottish publisher named Alexander Macmillan wrote to a friend asking whether he thought a one-volume edition of Shakespeare's plays, to be sold at a reasonable price of three shillings and sixpence ($19.00 today), would sell 50,000 copies in three years. It sold over a quarter of a million copies in the forty-seven years of its publication. The name Macmillan chose for it was *The Globe,* which was to encompass both Shakespeare's theater and the world. The editors of the Globe were the same two Cambridge University scholars, Clark and Wright. In his introduction to the Globe edition, Macmillan wrote:

> We trust that the title which has been chosen for the present edition will neither be thought presumptuous or be found inappropriate. It seems indeed safe to predict that any volume which presents in a convenient form with clear type and at a moderate cost, the complete works of the foremost man in all literature, the greatest master of the language most widely spoken among men, will make its way to the remotest corners of the habitable globe.[20]

The Globe edition is the source for all of Shakespeare's text published in this book and is found online as Open Source Shakespeare.

Modern Editions of Shakespeare

There is not one definitive Shakespearean text—even the First Folio has errors, lots of them. Shakespeare's scripts, even in his own time, changed with different productions and different actors. New scholarship and editorship brings change to existing texts. If you find that your sense of your character is at variance with the text you are given, check the Folio, check other texts, and note the variance in punctuation and word use, and you may find justification for your choice. For instance, in *The Tempest* in the First Folio and some editions, Prospero uses the word *mushrumps*, whereas in some editions he uses *mushrooms*. Possibly an Elizabethan audience would find *mushrumps* a more familiar word than *mushrooms*, which is the word every audience is familiar with today. Compare:

> and you, whose pastime
> Is to make midnight-**Mushrumps**, that rejoyce
> To heare the solemn Curfewe,
> *The Tempest* (First Folio) 5.1.1989–1991[21]

> and you whose pastime
> Is to make midnight **mushrooms**, that rejoice
> To hear the solemn curfew;
> *The Tempest* (Arden) 5.1.36–38[22]

Here is an example of a single exchange in different editions of *As You Like It*:

> CELIA. Prethee, who is't that thou means't?
> CLOWNE. One that old Fredericke your Father loves.
> ROSALIND. My Fathers love is enough to honor him enough; speake no more of him, you'l be whipt for taxation one of these daies.
> *As You Like It* (First Folio) 1.2.76–80[23]

Compare that to the version suggested by Helga Kokeritz, the editor of the Yale Edition:

> CELIA. Who is't that thou meanst?
>
> TOUCHSTONE. One that old Frederick, your father, loves.
>
> CELIA. My father's love is enough to honor him: enough! speak no more of him; you'll be whipped for taxation one of these days.[24]

Personally, I like the second sample as it gives the actress playing Celia a stronger reaction to Touchstone's snide comment about her father.

There are sometimes subtle textual differences between the Folio edition of Shakespeare and contemporary editions that only become apparent during the rehearsal of a play. In the summer of 2018, I was directing *Much Ado about Nothing* for the Prague Shakespeare Company's Summer Shakespeare Intensive, using a ninety-minute version I edited from Open Source Shakespeare. During the first week of the program, Eric Rasmussen, Shakespearean scholar and the editor of the Royal Shakespeare Company's *Complete Works of Shakespeare*, visited Prague and gave a lecture to the students about textual differences that can influence character choices found in the Folio and contemporary Shakespeare editions. As an example, he referenced the famous line from *Much Ado about Nothing* at the end of the play, when Beatrice and Benedick almost don't unite because they are so busy arguing and contradicting each other:

> BENEDICK. Soft and fair, friar. Which is Beatrice?
>
> BEATRICE. [*Unmasking*] I answer to that name. What is your will?
>
> BENEDICK. Do not you love me?
>
> BEATRICE. Why, no; no more than reason.
>
> BENEDICK. Why, then your uncle and the prince and Claudio Have been deceived; they swore you did.
>
> BEATRICE. Do not you love me?
>
> BENEDICK. Troth, no; no more than reason.
>
> BEATRICE. Why, then my cousin Margaret and Ursula Are much deceived; for they did swear you did.

BENEDICK. They swore that you were almost sick for me.
BEATRICE. They swore that you were well-nigh dead for me.
BENEDICK. 'Tis no such matter. Then you do not love me?
BEATRICE. No, truly, but in friendly recompense.

In all contemporary versions, Benedick stops the arguments by saying:

BENEDICK. Peace! I will stop your mouth. [*Kissing her*]

However, in the First Folio and in all of the early editions of *Much Ado*, both the 1600 quarto and the 1623 folio, the line is given to Leonato, Beatrice's uncle, who with other characters in the play has been trying to facilitate the match between the two.

LEONATO. Peace! I will stop your mouth.

According to Eric Rasmussen, the editor Lewis Theobald gave the line to Benedick in his 1733 edition and, "so far as I know, all editors since have followed in lock-step."

In rehearsal, I found that when Benedick said the line, it somehow didn't seem right. Instead of both Beatrice and Benedick being too stubborn to give in to each other, when Benedick said the line, it gave him a slight advantage because he ends the argument with a kiss. We decided to test what would happen when the line was given to Leonato as in the First Folio. It worked! As Beatrice and Benedick spoke their lines, they came closer and closer together, arguing, until they were facing each other directly. When the actor playing Leonato spoke the final line, I had him bring their heads together for a kiss. Everyone agreed that it quickly brought the argument to a joyous conclusion, with neither character having to give in to the other.

When I contacted Eric Rasmussen, he replied: "Delighted to hear that, Linda. I restored the line to Leonato in my RSC edition but otherwise Benedick has been delivering it for 300 years!"[25]

Shakespeare Online

When I set out to write this book, which evolved over the years from teaching young actors to speak Shakespeare's text, I discovered that I could access Shakespeare online—at no cost.

Monologues, scenes, and sonnets were easily available to me and my students. Having written my first book, *Voice for Performance*, initially on a typewriter, then rewritten it on a word processor, then scanned the typewritten pages to a computer, I was deeply grateful for the ease of access and availability. However, when I sent in the current volume as a manuscript to Northwestern University Press, I discovered that it was not so simple. Many editions of Shakespeare, even the Folger Shakespeare Library editions, are not in the public domain. Royalties for the amount of Shakespeare's text that I was using would be prohibitive.

Thankfully, there is the website Open Source Shakespeare, which compiles the public-domain Globe texts of all Shakespeare's plays into an easily accessible format. This site was the work of a young American Marine reservist, Eric M. Johnson,[26] who was serving with the American forces during the Iraq War after Baghdad fell. Johnson found himself sitting in a tent in the desert in Kuwait with time on his hands waiting for "contingencies." Before he was called to duty in Iraq, he had served as theater critic to the *Washington Times*, where he also worked during the day managing the paper's website operations.

Johnson was able to see quite a few productions of Shakespeare at the Folger Theatre and the Shakespeare Theatre Company, and being a conscientious reviewer, he actually read the plays before he saw them. When he needed a selection of Shakespeare's text to supplement his reviews, he went online to find and download them. Intrigued by the ease of accessing Shakespeare in this way, he began building a website with *As You Like It,* just to see if he could. Of course, juggling a demanding full-time job and a family didn't leave much time for further web building, so his "Shakespeare database project," as he called it, languished.

In Kuwait, as the weeks sitting in the desert dragged on, using his laptop and the Globe edition of Shakespeare, Johnson began to build what would become Open Source Shakespeare. It has been a wonderful resource for this book, and I am forever in his debt.

Today Arthur Macmillan's title *The Globe* is more accurate than he could have imagined. Clark and Wright's work of compiling Shakespeare's texts, first into the nine-volume Cambridge edition and then into the one-volume Globe edition—labor done with what we would now consider the "primitive" tools of pen, paper, and perhaps a typewriter—lives on in other collected works under the imprint of a wide variety of editors with new corrections and amendments. However, their original collection, as they originally conceived it, with all their corrections and amendments, now travels with the speed of the internet around the globe.

Shakespeare's Text Today

It is interesting that in the theater today there is more focus than there has been at any other time on performing Shakespeare's text as he wrote it. There are countless editions of Shakespeare, but the emphasis is the same: accuracy and the desire to present Shakespeare's text in the context of what he intended.

Like the many editors who worked on Shakespeare's text so it could be understood and enjoyed, an actor's goal should be to communicate Shakespeare's text to an audience so they can hear it and understand it. We in the English-speaking world are lucky that our greatest dramatist is also one of our greatest poets. It is helpful to know that Shakespeare has made our work as actors easier by incorporating the devices of rhetoric and verse into his dramatic texts so that, regardless of what edition we are using, the language itself holds the clues to guide us. The purpose of this book is to help actors develop an awareness of how Shakespeare's writing holds its own clues for performance, despite differences in punctuation and spelling, and to learn how to follow the rhetorical and poetic guides he has set down for us.

We owe a very great debt to Shakespeare's colleagues John Heminges and Henry Condell for their great labor of love in compiling Shakespeare's plays into the one-volume First Folio. No rehearsal of a Shakespeare play should take place without the Folio on the rehearsal table for the actors and directors to consult. It is the basis of all that came afterward. However, we also owe a debt to the scholarly work of the many editors who have worked tirelessly on Shakespeare's text over the last four hundred years. And finally a very special thanks to William George Clark and William Aldis Wright, whose enormous work of scholarship, largely unheralded, brought the Cambridge edition and then the Globe edition of Shakespeare forward, into what is now available to the world in Open Source Shakespeare.

I believe that actors and directors should also take full advantage of modern Shakespearean scholarship when working on the text. When rehearsing a character, if you feel that the punctuation in the edition you are using doesn't support what you are trying to convey, it can be helpful to consult not only the First Folio, but other editions as well for alternative punctuation choices. As Hamlet said to the actors he was coaching:

> Suit the action to the word, the word to the action; with this special observance, that you o'erstep not the modesty of nature: for anything so overdone is from the purpose of playing, whose end, both at the first and now, was and is, to hold, as 'twere, the mirror up to nature; to show Virtue her own feature, scorn her own image, and the very age and body of the time his form and pressure.
>
> *Hamlet*, 3.2.14–20

APPENDIX

Additional Shakespearean Texts

Monologues are usually performed by actors as audition pieces for jobs in the theater. Generally speaking, there are two types of monologues: the soliloquy and the direct address, which is a speech directed to another character or to the audience.

The term *soliloquy* comes from the Latin and means "talking to oneself." It is a device whereby Shakespeare allows his characters to share their innermost thoughts with the audience. If there are other characters on stage, they do not hear the soliloquy. In direct address the actor places the character being addressed in front of him or her. This allows the actor to direct the speech toward the auditioner, who is usually seated in front of the stage.

In the following selections both monologues and two-person scenes are provided as material for individual actors, both men and women. I've included scenes for two men, two women, and a man and a woman. It is certainly possible to do gender-flipped casting for both the monologues and two-person scenes. I've also provided the opening line and an introduction to each selection. Read to the end of the scene or stop where you see fit. You may use any edition of Shakespeare for the selections as long as both actors use the same text for two-person scenes. My students like to use Open Source Shakespeare, which they access on their phones.

Men's Monologues

Hamlet—Act 1, Scene 2 (Hamlet)

Beginning: O that this too too solid flesh would melt,

Hamlet—Act 2, Scene 2 (Hamlet)

Beginning: I have of late—but wherefore I know not—lost all my mirth, forgone

Here are two speeches from *Hamlet* spoken by the prince. One monologue is in verse and the other in prose. The first speech is a soliloquy—Hamlet is speaking to himself. In the second speech, Hamlet is speaking to his former classmates Rosencranz and Guildenstern to describe his state of mind.

Love's Labour's Lost—Act 3, Scene 1 (Biron)

Beginning: And I, forsooth, in love!

Four young men—Ferdinand, the King of Navarre, and his friends, the courtiers Biron, Longaville, and Dumain—have gathered together for three years to devote themselves to study and to shun the company of women. The character of Biron (in some editions called "Berowne") is speaking in a soliloquy. Notice how he uses the rhetorical devices of antithesis, wordplay, irony, alliteration, and assonance in his process of self-discovery.

King Lear—Act 1, Scene 2 (Edmund)

Beginning: Thou, Nature, art my goddess;

Edmund, the illegitimate son of the Duke of Gloucester, plots to deprive his legitimate brother Edgar of his land and life. He uses direct address to the audience, with alliteration—"Why brand they us / With base? With baseness? Bastardy base? Base?"—and wordplay on the word "legitimate."

Measure for Measure—Act 2, Scene 2 (Angelo)

Beginning: What's this, what's this? Is this her fault or mine?

Angelo is appointed ruler in the absence of the rightful Duke, and has begun to enforce strict laws against fornication. When a young man is condemned for getting his fiancée with child, his sister pleads with Angelo for his life. Angelo then discovers that he desires her and is just as susceptible as the young man he has sentenced to death. Notice the use of rhetorical questions.

Much Ado about Nothing—Act 2 Scene 3 (Benedick)

Beginning: I do much wonder that one man,

Benedick, having returned victorious from war to civilian life, is astonished that his young comrade Claudio is now more interested in falling in love than in military life and wonders whether he could be susceptible too. This monologue is in prose, but it employs the same rhetorical figures of antithesis, simile, and metaphor as found in verse.

Henry V—Act 1 Scene 2 (King Henry)

Beginning: We are glad the Dauphin is so pleasant with us;

The young King Henry V has just ascended to the throne and, in reply to a request for dukedoms in France, the French ambassador brings the King a denial from the Dauphin and a gift of tennis balls, mocking Henry's wilder days before he became king.

Henry IV, Part 1—Act 1, Scene 3 (Hotspur)

Beginning: My liege, I did deny no prisoners.

Henry Percy, nicknamed "Hotspur" because of his hot temper, is the son of the Earl of Northumberland, who is England's traditional protector. Hotspur is accused by King Henry IV of refusing to ransom his prisoners captured in a recent battle.

Troilus and Cressida—Act 5, Scene 2 (Troilus)

Beginning: This she? no, this is Diomed's Cressida:

In the middle of the Trojan War, two young Trojans, Troilus and Cressida, become lovers. The next day they learn that Cressida has been chosen for a prisoner exchange with the Greeks. That night an anguished Troilus sneaks into the Greek camp and sees Cressida flirt with Diomed, one of the Greek soldiers.

Othello—Act 2, Scene 3 (Iago)

Beginning: And what's he then that says I play the villain?

Iago has just counseled Cassio, a young soldier who has disgraced himself with drunkenness, to appeal to Othello's wife, Desdemona, to intercede for him, as a way to provoke Othello's jealousy. In this direct address to the audience, Iago challenges the audience to say he could be said to be doing wrong.

King John—Act 1, Scene 1 (Philip the Bastard)

Beginning: A foot of honour better than I was;

In *King John*, when Philip the Bastard is revealed to be the illegitimate son of Richard, Coeur-de-lion, he chooses to renounce his role as eldest son to the Duke of Faulconbridge and to follow Queen Eleanor of Aquitaine with her son King John to war in France.

The Tempest—Act 2, Scene 2 (Trinculo)

> **Beginning:** Here's neither bush nor shrub . . .

Trinculo has been shipwrecked with the entire crew on an enchanted island. As a storm threatens, he sees what he thinks to be a sea beast and decides to take cover under it.

Twelfth Night—Act 4, Scene 3 (Sebastian)

> **Beginning:** This is the air; that is the glorious sun;

Sebastian, the twin brother of Viola, has just met the Countess Olivia, who mistakes him for Caesario, a young follower of the Count Orsino, with whom she is in love. "Caesario" is really his twin sister Viola in disguise, whom he believes has drowned in a shipwreck. When Olivia asks Sebastian to marry her, he is astonished and realizes that the world around him isn't what he thinks it is.

Women's Monologues

Comedy of Errors, Act 2, Scene 2 (Adriana)

> **Beginning:** Ay, ay, Antipholus, look strange and frown:

Antipholus of Syracuse and his servant Dromio of Syracuse have just arrived by ship from Ephesus, setting off a series of mistaken identities. Adriana, the wife of Antipholus of Ephesus, accuses the man whom she believes to be her husband of betraying her with another woman. Unknown to her, he is her husband's twin brother, from whom he was separated in infancy.

All's Well That Ends Well—Act 3 Scene 2 (Helena)

Beginning: 'Till I have no wife, I have nothing in France.'

Helena, the adopted ward of the Countess of Rousillon, after having cured the King of France of a serious illness, is rewarded by the King by giving her in marriage to Bertam, the Countess's son. Bertram is not in love with Helena and, rather than consummate the marriage, he runs away to the wars vowing never to be her husband.

Merry Wives of Windsor—Act 2, Scene 1 (Mistress Page)

Beginning: What, have I scaped love-letters

Mistress Page, a happily married housewife in Windsor, has just received a love letter from Sir John Falstaff, a fat, lecherous, drunken nobleman, proposing a romantic assignation.

As You Like It—Act 3, Scene 5 (Phoebe)

Beginning: Think not I love him, though I ask for him;

Phoebe, a pretty young shepherdess, is pursued by Silvius, a young shepherd who she disdains. While Silvius pleads for her love, she berates him, until she is rudely interrupted by Ganymede, who is really Rosalind, a young woman recently arrived in the forest of Arden and disguised as a boy. When Rosalind, still pretending to be Ganymede, chastises Phoebe for her cruelty to Silvius, Phoebe instantly falls in love with Ganymede and, under the guise of pretending to be angry with him, persuades Silvius to act as a go-between in her pursuit of Ganymede.

Henry VI, Part 1—Act 5, Scene 3 (Joan La Pucelle)

Beginning: The regent conquers, and the Frenchmen fly.

When Joan la Pucelle (Joan of Arc) is losing the battle against the English forces, she calls upon her spirits to help her. They desert her and she is captured.

Henry IV, Part 2—Act 2, Scene 3 (Lady Percy)

Beginning: O, yet, for God's sake, go not to these wars!

Henry Percy, known as Hotspur, has been killed in battle by Henry V. His widow, Kate, bitterly reproaches her father-in-law for not joining in the battle as he had promised, thus leaving his son undefended. He has now proposed to continue the war and is planning another battle.

Richard III—Act 1, Scene 2 (Lady Anne)

Beginning: Foul devil, for God's sake, hence, and trouble us not;

Lady Anne, the widow of Prince Edward, is accompanying the body of her father-in-law King Henry VI when she encounters Richard, the Duke of Gloucester, who murdered both her husband and the King.

Romeo and Juliet—Act 2, Scene 2 (Juliet)

Beginning: Thou know'st the mask of night is on my face,

After meeting Juliet at the ball, Romeo climbs over the garden wall surrounding her house and overhears her declare her love for him. After he speaks to her of his love, she declares her love for him and asks if his intention is honorable marriage.

The Merchant of Venice—Act 3, Scene 2 (Portia)

Beginning: You see me, Lord Bassanio, where I stand,

Portia, a wealthy young noblewoman, is bound by the statutes of her father's will to marry only the man who could determine which of the three caskets—gold, silver, or lead—contained her picture. Bassanio, who is her desired choice, has opened the casket and guessed correctly. Portia now confronts her own feelings as she renounces her independence and gives herself into Bassanio's keeping.

Twelfth Night—Act 2, Scene 2 (Viola)

Beginning: I left no ring with her:

Viola is disguised as Caesario, a young gentleman in Count Orsino's court. Orsino is in love with the Countess Olivia and at his insistence sends Viola to woo Olivia for him. Olivia tells Viola she cannot love Orsino and requests that he cease his courtship. After Viola leaves, Olivia sends a ring by her servant Malvolio which reveals her love for Caesario.

Two Gentlemen of Verona—Act 4, Scene 4 (Julia)

Beginning: How many women would do such a message?

Julia and Proteus were in love before Proteus followed his friend Valentine to the royal court in Milan. On arriving at court, Proteus soon falls in love with Sylvia, who is the beloved of Valentine. When Proteus learns that Sylvia's father wants her to marry another man, he betrays his friend Valentine, who than flees for his life. Meanwhile, when Julia follows Proteus to the court, disguised as a boy, Proteus engages Julia to be his page and asks her to court Sylvia for him. Sylvia wants nothing to do with Proteus as she still loves Valentine.

A Midsummer Night's Dream—Act 1, Scene 1 (Helena)

> **Beginning:** How happy some o'er other some can be!

Helena laments in rhymed couplets that in spite of being just as fair as her friend Hermia, her lover Demetrius is in love with Hermia, who is running away to be married to Lysander. Helena resolves to betray Hermia's flight to Demetrius.

Henry VI, Part 3,—Act 1, Scene 1 (Queen Margaret)

> **Beginning:** QUEEN MARGARET. Enforced thee! art thou king, and wilt be forced?

Queen Margaret has just discovered that her husband, Henry VI, has bowed to pressure to entail the throne of England to the House of York, thereby disinheriting his own son.

Two-Person Scenes

Man and Woman

A Midsummer Night's Dream—Act I, Scene 1 (Lysander and Hermia)

> **Beginning:** LYSANDER. How now, my love! why is your cheek so pale?

Lovers Lysander and Hermia are left alone after Hermia's father demands that Theseus, King of Athens, agree that Hermia should marry Demetrius, his choice of a husband for her, be consigned to a convent, or else be executed. It is odd, therefore, that the first thing Lysander says to Hermia is to inquire why she is so upset. As she replies to his question, both speak in verse using wordplay, antithesis, and rhetorical questions; Hermia realizes that love can always be fraught with challenges, and is then prepared for the good news that they can run away together to marry.

All's Well That Ends Well—Act 1, Scene 1 (Parolles and Helena)

Beginning: PAROLLES. Are you meditating on virginity?

Helena, the ward of the Countess of Rousillon, puts up with Parolles, a cowardly, vain, braggart, because he is the companion to Bertram, with whom she is in love.

All's Well That Ends Well—Act 4, Scene 2 (Bertram and Diana)

Beginning: BERTRAM. They told me that your name was Fontibell.

Although Bertram is married to Helena, he runs away to join the wars in Italy, leaving their marriage unconsummated. While he is abroad, he woos Diana, a virtuous maid, and promises to marry her when his wife is dead. Diana, unknown to him, is helping his wife Helena to win him back by fulfilling his vow not to live with her until she has a child of him. Diana pretends to grant his request for an assignation, which Helena will fulfill.

Measure for Measure—Act 2, Scene 4 (Isabella and Angelo)

Beginning: ISABELLA. I am come to know your pleasure.

Angelo has been appointed ruler of the state by the Duke, leaving him in charge of the kingdom. In the Duke's absence, Angelo has enforced the law with regard to fornication, condemning Claudio for getting his fiancée pregnant. Isabella, Claudio's sister, a young nun, appeals to Angelo, who at their first meeting has fallen in love with her. Angelo requests that she return to learn whether her brother can be saved.

Measure for Measure—Act 3, Scene 1 (Claudio and Isabella)

Beginning: CLAUDIO. Now, sister, what's the comfort?

Claudio is a a young man condemned to death by Angelo, the deputy ruler of the city, for the crime of fornication. Isabella, his sister and a young nun, goes to see Angelo to try to save him. Angelo tells her that he might spare her brother if she yields him her virginity. She refuses and comes to prepare Claudio for death the next day.

Much Ado about Nothing—Act 4, Scene 1 (Benedick and Beatrice)

Beginning: BENEDICK. Lady Beatrice, have you wept all this while?

Beatrice's young cousin Hero has been denounced by her intended husband Claudio at the altar where they were to be married and accused of meeting another man the night before her wedding. Beatrice calls on Benedick to avenge her cousin.

The Merchant of Venice—Act 5, Scene 1 (Lorenzo and Jessica)

Beginning: LORENZO. The moon shines bright:

Jessica has stolen away from Shylock, her father, and is now married to Lorenzo. They sit in the garden and talk of their love. Music is playing in the background during much of the scene, and the lovers use rhetoric to express their feelings.

Romeo and Juliet—Act 2, Scene 2 (Romeo and Juliet)

Beginning: ROMEO. But, soft! what light through yonder window breaks?

Romeo climbs over the garden wall after meeting Juliet at a ball and reveals himself to her when he sees her on her balcony.

The Tempest—Act 3, Scene 1 (Ferdinand and Miranda)

Beginning: FERDINAND. There be some sports are painful,

Ferdinand, after being shipwrecked on a desert island, meets Miranda, the daughter of Prospero, the former Duke of Milan who rules the island. As part of Prospero's plan to bring the two of them together, he harshly orders Ferdinand to pile up logs.

Macbeth—Act 1, Scene 7 (Lady Macbeth and Macbeth)

Beginning: LADY MACBETH. He has almost supp'd: why have you left the chamber?

Lady Macbeth discovers that her husband has left the dinner party they are hosting for King Duncan. Macbeth confesses that he is having second thoughts about the murder of the King.

Pericles—Act 4, Scene 3 (Dionyza and Cleon)

Beginning: DIONYZA. Why, are you foolish? Can it be undone?

Cleon and Dionyza are rulers of a country that Pericles had saved from starvation. After a storm at sea in which his wife dies in childbirth, Pericles has entrusted his infant daughter Marina to them. Years later, after she is grown, she beomes a rival to their daughter, and they arrange to have her murdered. In this scene Cleon discovers that his wife has arranged Marina's murder.

Hamlet—Act 3, Scene 1 (Hamlet and Ophelia)

Beginning: HAMLET. Soft you now! / The fair Ophelia

Ophelia returns the gifts that Hamlet has given her, and Hamlet castigates her for not being honest with him.

Two Women

All's Well That Ends Well—Act I, Scene 3 (Helena and Countess)

Beginning: HELENA. What is your pleasure, madam?

The Countess of Rousillon tries to discover the reason for the sadness of her ward Helena, whom she suspects is in love with her son Bertram.

As You Like It—Act 3, Scene 2 (Celia and Rosalind)

Beginning: CELIA. Didst thou hear these verses?

Rosalind and Celia discuss the verses they have discovered hung about the forest of Arden, which seem to have been writen by an unknown admirer of Rosalind.

Othello—Act 4, Scene 3 (Emilia and Desdemona)

Beginning: EMILIA. How goes it now? he looks gentler than he did.

Desdemona and her maid Emilia discuss Othello's behavior and Emilia tells her what, in her opinion, is the reason husbands treat their wives badly.

The Comedy of Errors—Act 2, Scene 1 (Adriana and Luciana)

Beginning: ADRIANA. Neither my husband nor the slave return'd,

Adriana is unhappily married to Antipholus of Ephesus, who neglects her. Luciana, who is unmarried, encourages her to accept that men are ordained by nature to have power over women and it is the natural order of things.

Twelfth Night—Act 1, Scene 5 (Viola and Olivia)

Beginning: OLIVIA. Give me my veil: come, throw it o'er my face.

Viola, disguised as a young man called Cesario, courts the Countess Olivia on behalf of the Duke Orsino.

Two Gentlemen of Verona—Act 4, Scene 4 (Julia and Sylvia)

Beginning: JULIA. I pray you, be my mean

Julia, who is in love with Proteus, has disguised herself as a boy, and courts Sylvia for Proteus, who is in love with her.

Merchant of Venice—Act 1, Scene 2 (Portia and Nerissa)

Beginning: PORTIA. By my troth, Nerissa, my little body is aweary of this great world.

Portia complains to her maid Nerissa about the difficulties she finds in choosing a husband by the precepts of her father's will.

Romeo and Juliet—Act 2, Scene 5 (Juliet and the Nurse)

Beginning: JULIET. The clock struck nine when I did send the nurse;

Juliet is impatiently waiting for the nurse to return from meeting Romeo to arrange for their marriage. She finally arrives with good news.

Two Gentlemen of Verona—Act 1, Scene 2 (Julia and Lucetta)

Beginning: JULIA. But say, Lucetta, now we are alone,

Julia and her maid Lucetta spar in verse about the advantages and disadvantages of various young men who might aspire to be Julia's lover.

Two Men

Romeo and Juliet—Act 1, Scene 1 (Benvolio and Romeo)

Beginning: BENVOLIO. Good-morrow, cousin.

Romeo's infatuation with Rosaline, a young woman who disdains his love, is a concern to his family. His best friend Benvolio tries to get him to see reason. They speak in rhymed couplets.

As You Like It—Act 3, Scene 2 (Corin and Touchstone)

Beginning: CORIN. And how like you this shepherd's life, Master Touchstone?

Touchstone, the fool of the usurping Duke, has fled the court with the Duke's daughter and niece to seek refuge in the forest of Arden. He finds himself in conversation with Corin, a shepherd, about advantages and disadvantages of life in the country as opposed to the city.

Two Gentlemen of Verona—Act 1, Scene 1 (Valentine and Proteus)

> **Beginning:** VALENTINE. Cease to persuade, my loving Proteus:

Valentine is preparing to leave home for the royal court to improve his education and acquire sophistication. When his friend Proteus, who remains behind because of his love for Julia, tries to persuade him to remain at home, Valentine encourages Proteus to join him.

Julius Caesar—Act 4, Scene 3 (Cassius and Brutus)

> **Beginning:** CASSIUS. That you have wrong'd me doth appear in this:

Cassius complains to his friend Brutus that he is being treated unfairly and accuses Brutus of taking sides against him.

Two Gentlemen of Verona—Act 2, Scene 4 (Valentine and Proteus)

> **Beginning:** VALENTINE. Now, tell me, how do all from whence you came?

Proteus has arrived at court in Milan, where he is reunited with his friend Valentine and meets Valentine's new love Sylvia.

As You Like It—Act 3, Scene 2 (Jaques and Orlando)

> **Beginning:** JAQUES. I thank you for your company;

Jaques is one of the followers of the banished Duke who has taken refuge in the forest of Arden. He is addicted to an affectation of melancholy and enjoys speaking out against love. Orlando, a young man who has also taken refuge with the Duke, encounters Jaques in the forest, where they politely spar in verse as Orlando cheerfully declines to share a melancholy view of life.

Two Gentlemen of Verona—Act 1, Scene 1 (Speed and Proteus)

Beginning: SPEED. Sir Proteus, save you! Saw you my master?

This scene from *Two Gentlemen of Verona* between Proteus and Valentine's servant Speed uses lots of wordplay, including a pun on "shipp'd" and "sheep." In Shakespeare's Original Pronunciation these two words were pronounced alike. According to British linguist David Crystal:

> The close front vowel in sheep and the mid-close front vowel (of ship) are a very short distance from each other, phonetically, especially in accents (such as Scottish) where sheep is pronounced quite short. The two words that fuel a pun don't have to be phonetically identical. People get the joke, and so would an Elizabethan audience, as these two vowels have changed very little over the past four hundred years.

Giving Speed a Scottish or Original Pronunciation accent might make the scene a bit clearer for American audiences. The word play and puns are what makes this scene work and shouldn't be ignored. Actors should always look up the meaning for archaic words, such as "noddy" (stupid), "laced mutton" (prostitute), "testered" (present with a sixpence).

Romeo and Juliet—Act 2, Scene 3 (Romeo and the Friar)

Beginning: ROMEO. Good morrow, father

Romeo has come to ask the Friar's help in arranging his marriage with Juliet. The Friar is surprised because he thought Romeo was in love with Rosaline.

Hamlet—Act 4, Scene 7 (Claudius and Laertes)

Beginning: CLAUDIUS. What should this mean? Are all the rest come back?

Claudius (King Claudio) finds that Hamlet has escaped the death he arranged for him in England and is now returning to Denmark. He persuades Laertes to kill him in a duel.

NOTES

Introduction

1. Arthur Hornblow, *A History of the Theatre in America*, vol. 1 (Philadelphia: J. B. Lippincott, 1919).

2. "George Washington at the Theater," Mount Vernon Ladies' Association, accessed January 31, 2018, http://www.mountvernon.org/george-washington/colonial-life-today/entertaining-george-washington/.

3. Alexis de Tocqueville, *Democracy in America*, trans. and ed. Harvey C. Mansfield and Delba Winthrop (Chicago: University of Chicago Press, 2000), 445. Emphasis in the original.

4. John Bernard, *Retrospections of America, 1797–1811* (New York: Harper, 1887), 263.

5. Qtd. in Robert Walsh, *Didactics: Social, Literary, and Political*, vol. 1 (Freeport, N.Y.: Books for Libraries Press, 1972), 151.

6. Hornblow, *A History of the Theatre in America*, vol. 1.

7. Qtd. in Claudia Durst Johnson, *Church and Stage: The Theatre as Target of Religious Condemnation in Nineteenth-Century America* (Jefferson, N.C.: McFarland, 2008), 140. Emphasis in Johnson.

8. On the Macready-Forrest rivalry and the Astor Place riots, see David S. Reynold, *Walt Whitman's America: A Cultural Biography* (New York: Random House, 1995), 163; and Nigel Cliff, *The Great Shakespeare Riot* (New York: Random House, 2007), 15.

9. *Free Library*, "Ira Aldridge at Covent Garden, April 1833," accessed February 9, 2018, https://www.thefreelibrary.com/.

10. Bernth Lindfors, *Ira Aldridge: The African Roscius* (Rochester, N.Y.: University of Rochester Press, 2007).

11. Qtd. in Lawrence W. Levine, *Highbrow/Lowbrow: The Emergence of Cultural Hierarchy in America* (Cambridge, Mass.: Harvard University Press, 1988), 18.

12. Mark Twain, *Adventures of Huckleberry Finn* (New York: Charles L. Webster, 1885), 178–79.

13. Twain, *Adventures of Huckleberry Finn*, 199.

14. Lewis Clinton Strang, *Players and Plays of the Last Quarter Century*, vol. 1, *The Theatre of Yesterday* (Boston: L. C. Page, 1903), 68.

15. Qtd. in Jason Stacy, *Walt Whitman's Multitudes: Labor Reform and Persona in Whitman's Journalism and the First Leaves of Grass, 1840–1855* (New York: Peter Lang, 2008), 79.

16. Joseph Jefferson, *The Autobiography of Joseph Jefferson* (New York: Century, 1890), 30.

17. Abraham Lincoln, "President Lincoln on Shakespeare.; A LETTER TO MR. HACKETT." *New York Times*, September 20, 1863.

18. Douglas L. Wilson, "His Hour upon the Stage," *American Scholar*, November 30, 2011, https://theamericanscholar.org/his-hour-upon-the-stage/.

19. Barry Edelstein, "Shakespeare for Presidents," *New York Times*, April 25, 2009, http://www.nytimes.com/2009/04/26/weekinreview/26edelstein.html.

20. Karon Liu, "Nicolas Cage on Being a Believable Drug Addict and Why He Won't Do Shakespeare," *Toronto Life*, September 16, 2009, https://torontolife.com/culture/movies-and-tv/nicolas-cage-on-being-a-believable-drug-addict-and-why-he-wont-do-shakespeare/.

21. Tim Walker, "Trevor Nunn Says American Actors Can Get Closer to Shakespeare," *Telegraph*, October 9, 2009, http://www.telegraph.co.uk/culture/theatre/theatre-news/6280585/Trevor-Nunn-says-American-actors-can-get-closer-to-Shakespeare.html.

22. John Barton, *Playing Shakespeare: An Actor's Guide* (London: Methuen Drama, 1984), 6.

23. Harold Clurman, "The Famous 'Method,'" in *The Collected Works of Harold Clurman: Six Decades of Commentary on Theatre, Dance, Music, Film, Arts, and Letters*, ed. Marjorie Loggia and Glenn Young (New York: Applause Books, 1994), 371–72.

24. Clurman, "The Famous 'Method,'" 372.

25. John Gielgud, *An Actor and His Time* (New York: Applause Books, 1979), 130.

26. Michael Billington, "Henry IV, Parts One and Two," *Guardian*, July 13, 2006, https://www.theguardian.com/stage/2006/jul/13/theatre.rsc.

27. Qtd. in Andrea Grossman, "A Shakespearean Actor Prepares," transcribed by Kurt Wahlner, *WritersBloc*, April 16, 2001, http://www.writersblocpresents.com/archives/shakespeare/shakespeare.htm.

Chapter 1

1. Kristin Linklater, *Freeing Shakespeare's Voice* (New York: Theatre Communications Group, 1993).

2. A. L. Rowse, ed. *The Annotated Shakespeare: Hamlet* (New York: Greenwich House, 1988), 1761.

3. A. R. Braunmiller, ed. *The Tragical History of Hamlet, Prince of Denmark*, by William Shakespeare, Pelican Shakespeare (New York: Penguin Books, 2001), 65.

4. As related by George Hall, the former director of the acting program at the Royal Central School of Speech and Drama and vocal coach to Evans for her performance in *Hay Fever* at the Royal National Theatre. Email message to the author, March 9, 2018.

Chapter 3

1. Anthony Burgess, *A Mouthful of Air: Language and Languages, Especially English* (New York: William Morrow, 1993), 139.

2. *Beowulf*, trans. Francis B. Gummere (New York: P. F. Collier, 1910), prelude, lines 1–11.

Chapter 4

1. Wilbur Samuel Howell, *Logic and Rhetoric in England* (New York: Russell and Russell, 1961), 3.

2. Maria Perry, *The Word of a Prince: A Life of Elizabeth I from Contemporary Documents* (Rochester, N.Y: Boydell Press, 1999), 198.

3. Elizabeth I. *Collected Works*, edited by Leah S. Marcus, Janel Mueller, and Mary Beth Rose (Chicago: University of Chicago Press, 2000), 325–26.

4. "Elizabeth R Part 5" (BBC 1971) *The Enterprise of England*, YouTube.com, published by otchyanis on December 22, 2012. No longer available on YouTube but still can be found online, various sources.

5. "Virginia: Old Dominion," *World Book Encyclopedia*, 2001.

6. Patrick Fraser Tytler, *Life of Sir Walter Raleigh* (London: T. Nelson, 1849), 365.

7. Tytler, *Life of Sir Walter Raleigh*, 357.

8. Account attributed to Edward Hall's *Chronicle* (1548). Qtd. in Alison Weir, *The Lady in the Tower: The Fall of Anne Boleyn* (Toronto: McClelland and Stewart, 2010), 281.

9. Elizabeth Benger, *Memoirs of the Life of Anne Boleyn, Queen of Henry VIII*, 3rd ed. (London: Longman, Rees, Orme, Brown, and Green, 1827), 424.

10. Mary Cowden Clarke, ed., *Shakespeare's Works* (New York: D. Appleton, 1872), xxviii–xxix.

11. "Ben Jonson," *Grolier Encyclopedia of Knowledge*, 1991.

12. Sister Miriam Joseph, *Shakespeare's Use of the Arts of Language* (New York: Columbia University Press, 1947), 11.

13. Joseph, *Shakespeare's Use of the Arts of Language*, 11.

14. This list is based on that offered by Edward P. J. Corbett in *Classic Rhetoric for the Modern Student*, 3rd ed. (New York: Oxford University Press, 1990).

15. *Beowulf*, trans. Francis B. Gummere (New York: P. F. Collier, 1910), chapter 13, lines 848–50.

16. Gary Logan, *The Eloquent Shakespeare* (Chicago: University of Chicago Press, 2008).

17. David Crystal, *The English Language* (London: Penguin Books, 1988), 201.

18. David Crystal, email message to the author, September 24, 2017.

Chapter 6

1. Harley Granville-Barker, *Prefaces to Shakespeare: A Midsummer Night's Dream, The Winter's Tale, Twelfth Night* (1914; London, Nick Herne Books, 1993).

2. Drew Licthenberg, qtd. in an email message from Alan Paul to the author, March 5, 2018.

3. Barbara Gaines, email message to the author, March 6, 2018.

4. Ann Thompson, "The First and Second Quartos of *Hamlet*," British Library, accessed March 5, 2018, https://www.bl.uk/treasures /shakespeare/hamlet.html.

5. *The First Folio of Shakespeare 1623, Facsimile*, ed. Doug Moston (New York: Applause Books, 1993), 3.

6. George Puttenham, *The Art of English Poesie 1589* (London: Richard Field, 1589), 77.

7. David Crystal, *Think on My Words: Exploring Shakespeare's Language* (Cambridge: University of Cambridge Press, 2008), 68.

8. *The First Folio of Shakespeare 1623*, prepared and introduced by Doug Moston (New York: Applause Books, 1995).

9. This extract comes from Folger Digital Texts. Retrieved from www.folgerdigitaltexts.org.

10. David Crystal, *The Cambridge Encyclopedia of the English Language* (Cambridge, Cambridge University Press, 1995), 67.

11. *Benjamin Franklin's Autobiography: An Authoritative Text, Backgrounds, Criticism*, ed. J. A. Leo Lemay and P. M. Zall (New York: W. W. Norton, 1986), 5.

12. Barbara Gaines, email message to the author, March 6, 2018.

13. *Catharine and Petruchio: A Comedy, in Three Acts. As It Is Perform'd at the Theatre-Royal in Drury-Lane. Alter'd from Shakespear's Taming of the Shrew* (London: Joseph Thomas, 1838), 21. This adaptation by Garrick of *The Taming of the Shrew* first appeared in 1754 and held the stage for over a hundred years.

14. Barbara A. Murray, *Restoration Shakespeare: Viewing the Voice* (Madison, N.J.: Fairleigh Dickinson University Press, 2001), 306.

15. Victoria Joynes, "Into the Eighteenth Century: Shakespeare in Performance," *Shakespeare Birthplace Trust*, Explore Shakespeare (blog), May 6, 2016, https://www.shakespeare.org.uk/explore-shakespeare/blogs/18th-century-shakespeare-performance/.

16. *Catharine and Petruchio: A Comedy, in Three Acts. As It Is Perform'd at the Theatre-Royal in Drury-Lane. Alter'd from Shakespear's Taming of the Shrew*, ed. David Garrick (London: printed for J. and R. Tonson, and S. Draper, 1756). *The Taming of the Shrew*, ed. H. J. Oliver, 1982. *The Oxford Shakespeare* (Oxford: Oxford University Press), 65–70.

17. Marsden, Jean I. *The Re-imagined Text: Shakespeare, Adaptation, and Eighteenth-Century Literary Theory* (Lexington: University Press of Kentucky, 1995), 160.

18. Solveig Robinson, *The Book in Society: An Introduction to Print Culture* (Toronto: Broadview Press, 2014), 158.

19. Carrie Smith, "Battling over Eighteenth-Century Rights to Shakespeare," Folger Shakespeare Library, *The Collation: Research and Exploration at the Folger* (blog), October 13, 2011, https://collation.folger.edu/2011/10/battling-over-18th-century-rights-to-shakespeare/.

20. "The Farm Boy and the Nonconformist: A History of the Globe Shakespeare," Open Source Shakespeare, accessed March 5, 2018, https://www.opensourceshakespeare.org/info/about_the_texts.php.

21. *The First Folio of Shakespeare 1623* (New York: Applause Books, 1995).

22. Frank Kermode, ed., *The Tempest*, by William Shakespeare, Arden Edition of the Works of William Shakespeare (London: Routledge, 1988), 115.

23. *The First Folio of Shakespeare 1623* (New York: Applause Books, 1995).

24. *Comedies, Histories, and Tragedies (Facsimile of First Folio Edition of Shakespeare)*, edited by Helga Kokeritz and Charles Tyler Prouty (New Haven, Conn.: Yale University Press, 1954).

25. Email to author, July 14, 2018.

26. "Introduction: The History of Open Source Shakespeare," accessed March 7, 2018, https://www.opensourceshakespeare.org/info/aboutsite.php.